EARTH SCIENCES

AN ILLUSTRATED HISTORY OF PLANETARY SCIENCE

PONDERABLES™
100
DISCOVERIES
THAT CHANGED HISTORY
WHO DID WHAT WHEN

EARTH SCIENCES

AN ILLUSTRATED HISTORY OF PLANETARY SCIENCE

Tom Jackson

SHELTER HARBOR PRESS
NEW YORK

Contents

Introduction

WHAT BETTER SUBJECT TO STUDY THAN THE EARTH ITSELF? NOT ONLY IS IT OUR SOLE HOME, BUT IT IS ALSO FILLED WITH A GREAT MANY NATURAL WONDERS, FAR TOO NUMEROUS TO MENTION. IN ADDITION, AN EARTH SCIENTIST HAS A LOT OF SUBJECTS TO CHOOSE FROM. THEY COULD FATHOM THE MYSTERIES OF THE DEEP, DARK OCEAN, TRACK CHAOTIC WEATHER SYSTEMS LIKE HURRICANES AND TORNADOES, OR SEARCH OUT SOLID FACTS ABOUT THE ROCKS BENEATH OUR FEET.

No ordinary map of Britain, this one from 1815 shows the layers of rock types that make up the island. This was a first step to figuring out different ways rocks form and revealing the age of Earth.

In 1755 an earthquake and tsunami destroyed Lisbon, Portugal. Earth sciences are dealing with unimaginably huge and destructive forces.

The thoughts and deeds of great thinkers always make great stories, and here we have one hundred all together. Each story relates a ponderable, a weighty problem that became a breakthrough and changed the way we understand the planet, its ocean, and atmosphere. By understanding Earth, we also learn more about the rest of the Universe. However, knowledge does not arrive fully formed. We have to work at it, taking it in turns to consider the evidence and offer our take on what is true and what is not.

IT TAKES A WORLD

The story of earth sciences begins at the very start of the story of all science. Ancient thinkers who wanted to understand, well, everything there was to know, started with what they saw around them—the rocks of Earth, the water of the oceans, and air and winds in the sky.

This kind of thinking eventually led to the foundations of sciences such as physics and chemistry, which would later provide crucial understanding for all fields, but especially the earth sciences. However, already earth scientists were carving our their own areas of expertise. As can be expected, initial research arose from the need for practical benefits of knowledge, and so from China to the Mediterranean, the world's first weather forecasters began making predictions. Meanwhile, an interest in rocks arose because being good at finding valuable ores and gems has never been a bad idea.

Strabo's map of his known world in the 1st century CE stretched between India in the east and Portugal in the west. There was more to Earth than that, surely?

Left: In 1802, Luke Howard set up the system we still use to classify clouds. Here we see a cumulostratus.

Right: The members of the Southern Cross expedition of 1898 were the first to experience life in Antarctica during winter.

Meanwhile, Eratosthenes used mathematics to calculate a size for the planet. He was not far wrong, despite working 2,200 years ago with his only real piece of equipment being a column that cast a long shadow. A few centuries later, geographers like Strabo and Pytheas set out to descrbe the world in all of its richness. Starting small, the known world has grown in size. Seafarers told tall tales of far-off lands, and explorers like Leif Erikson, Zheng He, and Ferdinand Magellan risked life and limb to put them on the map.

MANY SCIENCES TOGETHER

By the end of the 16th century, the map of Earth was largely complete. But there were still many questions about how it came to be, what it was made of, and whether it was changing. Answers were only just beginning to emerge. Soon earth sciences would be clearly delineated into a set of separate disciplines: meteorologists study atmospheric effects, most notably the weather. Climatologists take a longer view and wonder how the conditions on Earth vary year to year or century to century—and chill out occasionally into ice ages. Meanwhile, oceanographers plumb the depths to figure out what is down at the bottom of the sea. Geology, the study of Earth itself, became divided into mineralogy and petrology, which seeks to understand naturally ocurring chemicals and how they form rocks. Geodicists make detailed measurements of the shape of Earth—it's not as round as you might think it is— while geophysicists want to know how the large-scale features of the planet—the mountains, the

ice caps, canyons, and deep ocean trenches—all fit into the global system. Two fields of study that have provided crucial contributions to these big-picture problems are seismology and paleontology. The former literally listens to the planet, and uses the sound-like seismic waves that rumble around inside to build a detailed picture of Earth's interior. The second—fossil hunting to you and me—allows us to date rocks and compare and contrast them with others from different parts of the world and different times in the long history of the planet. That is a powerful tool to help write the history of Earth. All this relies on a simple idea put forward in the 1830s by Charles Lyell, a leading figure in establishing the earth sciences of today. He said, "The present is the key to the past." If we look at what is happening on Earth right now, we will understand what happened to it in the past. And just as importantly, we will be able to predict with confidence what the future holds for Earth and all that live on it.

The Rosalind Franklin rover will be the first drilling rig on Mars, literally taking earth sciences out of this world.

Anatomy of the Earth

The largest of the rocky planets in our Solar System, Earth orbits the Sun once every year (365 days) and rotates in a west to east direction every 24 hours. around a north–south axis. While the poles are stationary relative to this axis, the equatorial regions are moving at more than 1,600 km/h (1,000 mph).

A layered planet

As it formed 4.5 billion years ago, Earth differentiated into layers, with the heavy metals deeper than the lighter rock. Temperatures rise with depth: the inner core is 4,700°C (8,500°F).

Atmospheric layers (see more, page 79):

Exosphere

Thermosphere

Mesosphere

Stratosphere

Troposphere

Upper mantle
(solid rock)
Depth from the
surface: 5–70 km
(3–45 miles)

Lower mantle
(solid rock)
Depth: 2,990 km
(1,860 miles)

Outer core
(liquid metal)
Depth: 5,150 km
(3,200 miles)

Inner core
(solid metal)
Depth: 6,370 km
(3,960 miles)

(see more,
page 89)

Continental crust
Thickness: up to
70 km (45 miles)

Oceanic crust:
Thickness: up to
5 km (3 miles)

Dividing lines

Earth is divided into a Northern and a Southern Hemisphere by the Equator. Earth's axis, which runs from pole to pole through the center of the planet, is tilted at around 23.5° to the vertical. As a result, the Sun shines more (and for longer each day) on the Northern Hemisphere for half a year, and then more on the Southern Hemisphere for the other half of the year. The Tropic of Cancer marks where the Sun is overhead when the daylength is longest in the Northern Hemisphere. The Tropic of Capricorn does the same in the south.

Cycle of Seasons

The tilt of Earth's axis creates the seasons. Summer occurs when the Sun is over the tropic in your hemisphere. Winter happens when it is above the tropic in the other hemisphere. Fall and spring are the periods of transition between these two extremes. The midway points are the equinoxes. These are two days a year, one in spring and one in fall, when the Sun is directly above the Equator, and night and day are the same length all over the world.

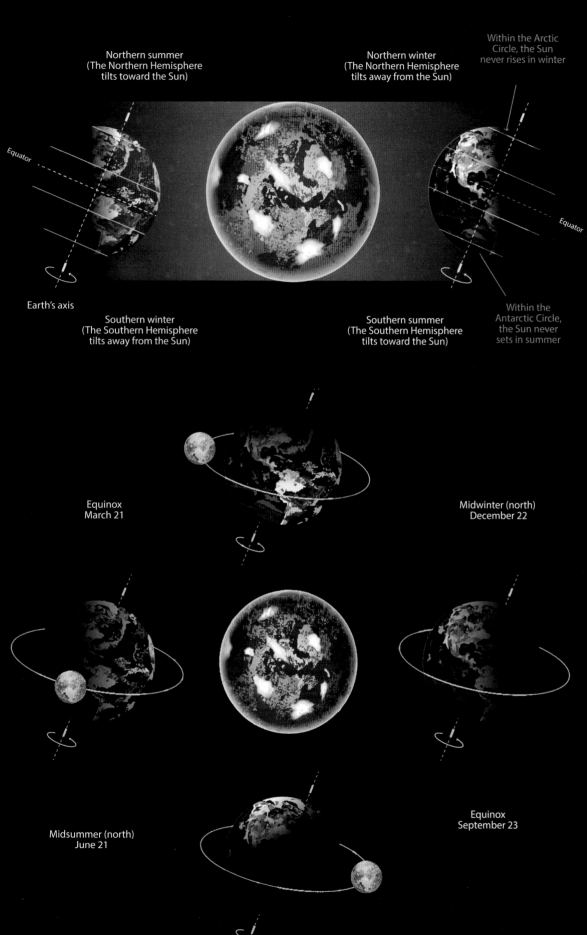

Northern summer
(The Northern Hemisphere tilts toward the Sun)

Northern winter
(The Northern Hemisphere tilts away from the Sun)

Within the Arctic Circle, the Sun never rises in winter

Equator

Earth's axis

Southern winter
(The Southern Hemisphere tilts away from the Sun)

Southern summer
(The Southern Hemisphere tilts toward the Sun)

Equator

Within the Antarctic Circle, the Sun never sets in summer

Equinox
March 21

Midwinter (north)
December 22

Midsummer (north)
June 21

Equinox
September 23

1 Seasons and Cycles

IF YOU ARE NOT A FARMER IT IS PERHAPS HARD TO FATHOM THE IMPORTANCE OF THE CHANGE IN WEATHER. In ancient times, everyone was a farmer, and knowledge of the seasons has formed the cornerstone of our civilizations.

Every culture has its feast days, perhaps commemorating an event in mythology or religious history. They have often become themed around a personal or societal goal, a struggle between good and evil of some kind. However, we could also understand these great days as a struggle between light and dark. Midwinter festivals mark the darkest time of the year, a period of celebration that the cold season is transitioning toward longer, warmer days. Spring festivals focus on preparing for the crucial growing season, using up the last of the perishable produce, and husbanding resources before the lean weeks of waiting for the first crops. And fall festivals, occurring in a time of relative plenty, acknowledge the return of the dark time and confront fears of the unknown as we head into winter.

The Intihuatana at the Inca city of Machu Pichu, Peru, is a sacred carved rock also known as the "Hitching Post of the Sun." Its exact function is unclear, but it is thought to be some kind of clock or calendar that traces the movements of the Sun and other astronomical objects to determine auspicious days and the correct times for important rituals (which included the sacrifice of children …)

THE DAWN OF METEOROLOGY

In Hindu mythology, the god Indra, the lord of the heavens (seen below on his elephant Airavata), is responsible for the weather—often using it to teach us mortals a lesson. Some of the earliest religious texts of all are the Hindu Upanishads, which date from 5,000 years ago. As well outlining the nature of the Universe and the pantheon of deities, these writings contain the earliest examples of meteorology, with discussions on the formation of clouds and the associated climatic shifts. with the changing seasons.

Measuring day lengths

The cultural year and the agricultural plan run hand in hand, both anchored to the calendar as developed in the earliest days of civilizations. Farmers must respond to changes in growing conditions, and these conditions are linked to the seasons, most specifically the way that days and nights vary in length. Lohri, Christmas, and Hanukkah are all dated to coincide with the winter solstice of the Northern Hemisphere, when day length is shortest. The various midsummer festivals occur in June when the day length is longest. Easter, Halloween, or Devali are festivals of the equinoxes, when the night length is equal to the day length. Beneath these traditions lies our intrinsic link to our planet, and that is the foundation of the great range of research areas we call the earth sciences.

2 Four Elements

THE IDEA THAT THE NATURAL WORLD AROUND US, WITH ITS DIVERSITY OF MATERIALS, is assembled from a set of simpler substances is an intuitive one. Ancient theories kept the idea very simple indeed.

A modern chemist will tell you that there are 90 elements found naturally on Earth, although a handful are in such minute quantities that their presence is mostly theoretical. (A further 28 have been created artificially.) The idea of an element—a substance that cannot be simplified into further ingredients—is at least 3,500 years old. Ancient cultures proposed variants of a short list comprising earth, water, air, metal, wood, and fire. However, it was the Greek list of four elements that dominated Western scientific thought until the end of the 18th century. In the 5th century BCE, the Greek philosopher Empedocles summed it up nicely in his poem *On Nature*: "Hear first the four roots of all things: Bright Zeus, life-giving Hera and Hades, and Persephone who moistens mortal springs with her tears." Zeus, the king of the gods, is the fire of the heavens, his wife Hera is the air of the sky. Hades, the lord of the underworld, represents earth, while Persephone (and her water) are imprisoned by Hades for half a year before being released in spring to allow life to return to the fields.

Empedocles lived at a time when what we now call "Western thought" was in its infancy, and was influenced by "Eastern" ideas, such as reincarnation. Empedocles believed he could escape the cycle of rebirth by accruing knowledge, and to prove it he jumped into Mount Etna. The volcano swallowed him up but spat out one shoe.

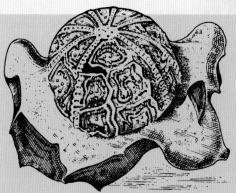

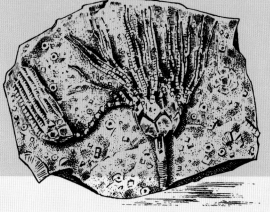

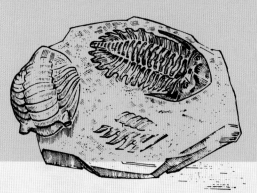

WATER WORLD

Empedocles was building on ideas from a first generation of Greek natural philosophers, led by Thales, who proposed that all materials and natural phenomena were formed from water, as the primal substance. Thales's contemporary Xenophanes saw that the remains of seashells and other marine life were fossilized in rocks far inland—even up mountains. To him, this backed up Thales's theory. It also suggested that Earth's surface was once covered in water, and had undergone great change in the unrecorded past.

Marine fossils as a feature of rocks far inland are evidence that the planet has changed in the past. Is it changing now?

3 Plato's Catastrophes

As a philosopher, Plato was more interested in the boundary between the real and unreal than figuring out how Earth worked. However, his writings record one of the greatest geological events of antiquity.

In his writings about the perfect society, *The Republic*, Plato referred to a lost land where such a society once existed. This was Atlantis, a vast island which harbored an advanced civilization. Plato told us an earthquake made the whole place slip beneath the sea—leaving an ocean we have come to call the Atlantic. The destructive powers of the Earth are truly awesome, although Plato's account was somewhat embellished. Later scholarship suggests that Atlantis was actually Akrotiri, a city on the island of Santorini, which was part of the Minoan culture centered on Crete in the eastern Mediterranean Sea. Much of Santorini (and Akrotiri with it) was destroyed in a volcanic eruption in the 16th century BCE, 1,250 years before Plato's retelling.

4 Aristotle's *Meteorologica*

While Plato focused on ideas, his pupil Aristotle wanted to understand by observing the world. Aristotle's approach formed the foundation of meteorology, as it did with several other sciences.

In about 350 BCE, after Aristotle had succeeded Plato as the most influential thinker of his day—and for the next millennium, at least—he wrote the *Meteorologica*, generally referred to as Aristotle's *Meteorology*. The title means "the study of meteors," which, confusingly, has a literal meaning in modern English, albeit an incorrect one. By *meteors*, Aristotle means atmospheric phenomena—weather, in all but name—but in his day that also included shooting stars. Today we know that these brief flashes of light in the night sky are astronomical phenomena, caused by grains of dust (or occasionally larger objects) entering the atmosphere from space. Confusingly, meteors are one thing that a modern meteorologist does not study.

Aristotle argued that rapid and constant changes in natural conditions, like lightning, were the result of elements separating into a pure state.

As well as the weather, *Meteorology* touches on all fields of earth science, such as geology, geodesy (the shape of Earth), and hydrology, which is concerned with the location and motion of water. For instance, Aristotle saw that rivers flowed and

INTO THE DEEP

Aristotle's legacy is rivaled by few. As well as inventing almost every science, he also mentored Alexander the Great, empire-builder extraordinaire. It is said that using a description from his teacher of the way sponge divers maximized time submerged, Alexander used diving bells in 332 BCE to send saboteurs to destroy the sea defenses of Tyre (now in Lebanon). Alexander is said to have made an exploratory dive himself (right), reckoned by some to be the first oceanographic expedition (but rumors he used a glass bell are entirely unfounded).

smaller regions of the sea had an obvious current, but a wider understanding of how water circulated was beyond his ability to observe.

Elemental forces

We still refer to the weather—especially the bad type—as "the elements," and Aristotle would approve. *Meteorology* was really concerned with understanding how nature was in a state of constant change. Aristotle's theory was that this flux of nature was driven by a fundamental battle between the four elements. Every natural change was the result of each element searching to find its correct level. Earth formed the lowest level, as evidenced by the land and seabed. Next came water, which covered the rocky surface, and then the air, which created the sky, and finally there was a ring of fire, which formed the boundary between heaven and Earth and was located just this side of the Moon.

This simple idea was highly compelling because it tallied so well with rudimentary observations. For example, when it rained, that was water separating from air and falling to its correct position. Flashes of lightning (and the streaks of meteors) was fire releasing itself from the air. Wood burned because it was a mixture of fire, air, and earth. The fire came out as flames, the air was the smoke, and the remaining ash was the earthly content. Eventually, Aristotle said, all four elements would separate completely, creating a perfect end point to history. The philosophical argument turned to whether any mixing processes balanced out the separations, but scientific debates pondered the inconsistencies in the theory. For example, if burning is the release of a substance, why do some materials get heavier? Aristotle's true legacy is that science has proved him wrong.

A SPHERICAL WORLD

Aristotle's concept of a layered world was based on the planet being a sphere. The sphere appealed to the ancient Greeks because of the harmony and apparent simplicity of its geometry. However, Aristotle pointed out real evidence that our planet was a globe: ships disappear below the horizon, hull first and mast last, as the surface of the planet curves away from the observer. More significantly, the shadow of Earth on the Moon during an eclipse is always circular. No shape other than a sphere always and only throws a circular shadow.

5 Voyage of Pytheas

IN OUR SMALL MODERN WORLD, ADVENTURERS OFTEN HAVE TO INVENT A GOAL TO CONQUER. Their forebear, Pytheas, did much the same thing 2,350 years ago when he went in search of all the world's cold. He said he found it at an island made of ice, which he named Thule.

This fresco uncovered from the ruins of Pompeii, a Roman city buried by a volcano in 79 CE, shows the globe with a mountain at the North Pole, thought to represent the source of cold, and later interpreted as a magnetic mountain.

The four classical elements were understood to embody more than just a physical property. Different cultures put store in their emotional and magical qualities. When it came to the weather and other natural processes, hot and cold were a crucial factor. The ultimate source of heat would obviously be the Sun, and the harmony imperative in Greek thought suggested that cold would arise in the opposite place—the center of the Earth.

In 325 BCE, a Greek explorer called Pytheas, hailing from Mediterranean colony of Massalia, now better known as Marseille, France, set off to find where all this cold came to the surface. The chill of the north wind suggested that was the direction to look in. First he went to what he called Bretannike—the first use of the name that eventually became Britain. (Word sleuths suggest that the root of this word is found in Welsh—the language closest to that of ancient Britain—and it means something like "land of the tattooed people," which remains an apt description.) Pytheas did not discover Britain, there were already strong tin-trade links with it, but he added it to the map of northwest Europe as he continued north from Scotland by ship. This took him all the way to Thule, a place where the sea was frozen and where the Sun never set—a phenomenon only visible above the Arctic Circle. Scholars wonder where he actually went, but the best bet is he swung eastward and made landfall in the far north of Norway.

The isle of Thule is still seen in this detail from a 16th-century world map, a version of a map first compiled in the 2nd century CE. According to this chart, Thule is northwest of the Orkney archipelago, islands just north of the British mainland.

6 On Stones

ARISTOTLE'S SUCCESSOR WAS HIS PUPIL THEOPHRASTUS, WHO became head of the Peripatetic school on his teacher's death. Luckily for him, there were still a few scientific fields left for him to found.

Like Aristotle before him, Theophrastus of Eresus had attended the Akademia, the open-air classroom in a walled-off olive grove on the edge of Athens where Plato taught his pupils. We get the English term *academy* from this ancient seat of learning. In middle age, Aristotle split with the ailing Plato and set up his own school, a movable institution that strolled as one in and around the Lycea, a temple to the wolf-form of the god Apollo. As such, Aristotle's school became known as the Lyceum. This is the root of the French word *lycée*, which means "high school." The nimble-footed students of the Lyceum, now joined by Theophrastus, became known as the Peripatetic school of philosophy, a name that now means "moving around."

The ancient Greeks were as into bling as anyone, as we can see from this golden seahorse brooch with an eye of polished carnelian. This stone is a red form of quartz frequently mis-described as ruby. In his book, Theophrastus explains how gold is a product of water, because both are able to flow.

New sciences

Theophrastus took over from Aristotle in 322 BCE, and along with works of literature and poetry, he left his mark as the founding figure in botany, the science of plants, and later with his book *On Stones*, which was the first attempt to classify rocks, minerals, and—most important among them—gemstones. This is no mean task. There are around 3,000 minerals described today, and 300 rocks which are composed of a selection of these minerals in varying proportions. Since Theophrastus was constrained by the notion that such materials were all made from earth, perhaps with some fire, water, and air mixed in, he did not differentiate clearly between rock and mineral.

Much of the text was devoted to where one might find the stone in question, and he paid particular attention to "stones of attraction," or magnets, and gems, which would have been of most interest to the reader. However, Theophrastus did set up a list of identifying characteristics for describing minerals which still largely hold to this day (along with several newer ones). These included hardness, color, and texture (or smoothness). He also took account of melting points, relative weights, and the impact of moisture or drying on the crystals.

THE BOOK OF SIGNS

Theophrastus was the author of an early book on weather forecasting called *The Book of Signs*. Published a few years after Aristotle's *Meteorology*, it built on Aristotle's teachings in an attempt to predict weather changes—handy since he and his fellow philosophers were outside so much. The signs Theophrastus noted included halos around the Sun and thickness and altitude of clouds which, combined with wind direction and temperature, signaled an impending change in weather. Like the work of his teacher, Theophrastus's system was largely guesswork.

7 The Circumference of the Earth

THE DEBATE OVER THE SHAPE OF THE EARTH WAS MORE OR LESS OVER BY THE 3RD CENTURY BCE. THERE WAS NO NEED TO FLY INTO SPACE TO LOOK: it was a sphere. A more interesting question was how big was the sphere. At the end of that century, the philosopher Eratosthenes saw a way to find an answer.

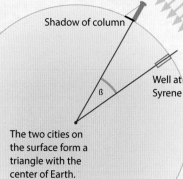

Column at Alexandria

Shadow of column

The Sun's rays are assumed to be parallel.

Well at Syrene

ß

The two cities on the surface form a triangle with the center of Earth.

As head of the Library of Alexandria, at the time the preeminent seat of learning in the world, Eratosthenes had the world's knowledge at his disposal. Every time a trader arrived in the city, they were required by law to leave whatever texts they had with the library (and had to make do themselves with a copy). Eratosthenes heard tell of a well near the city of Syrene (now Aswan) directly south of Alexandria, along the Nile River. On midsummer's day, the Sun shone straight down this well, and the walls cast no shadows. Eratosthenes knew that on the same day in Alexandria, the Sun did cast a shadow. This showed him that the Sun's rays were arriving at the two cities at different angles, and that would allow him to calculate what fraction of Earth's entire circumference was made up by the distance from Alexandria to Syrene.

Eratosthenes used the different angles of the Sun's rays to construct a triangle that connected the cities of Alexandria and Syrene to the center of the globe. The triangle's angle ß was the same as the angle of the Sun's rays at Alexandria, and that was the first step in showing what fraction of the total circumference was under consideration. The next step was to confirm how far it was from Alexandria to Syrene.

SEA LEVEL THEORY

While he did reveal the vast scale of Earth, Eratosthenes's geological theory was somewhat parochial. He explained the existence of fossilized shellfish on dry land by suggesting that the level of the Mediterranean Sea was once much higher, and it had dropped suddenly when two seaways opened up— what is now the Straits of Gibraltar leading to the Atlantic, and the Bosphorus (below), which links to the Black Sea.

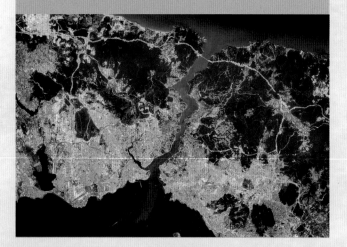

Data collection

Eratosthenes set up a column in Alexandria to measure the angle of the sunlight on the alloted day. It was about 7°, which is about a fiftieth of a full circle. He then consulted with merchants who took caravans to Syrene about how long it took to get there. That told him the distance was 5,000 stadia (the length of an athletics arena), and so Earth's circumference was about 250,000 stadia. In modern units, his final result was a globe 39,690 km (24,662 miles) around, not far wrong. Today's figure for the equivalent distance around the globe through the Poles is 40,008 km (24,860 miles).

8 *Geographica* by Strabo

SCIENTISTS GENERALLY TAKE A DIM VIEW OF GEOGRAPHY; IT LACKS THE RIGOR OF PHYSICS AND CHEMISTRY, they say. Strabo, the founding figure of the science, would agree—and he wanted it that way.

Strabo was a Pontic Greek, meaning he lived in what is now Turkey. He was inspired by the work of Eratosthenes and other earth scientists who used mathematics and rigorous observations to unlock knowledge about the planet. However, Strabo wanted to take a different approach. In 7 BCE he published the first of the 17 volumes of what would become *Geographica*. (The final book was released in 23 CE.) Strabo's aim was to write a book for travelers, ambassadors, and rulers which set out not only the physical features of the world's territories, but also facts about the people that lived there, and the difference between cultures.

Evolving world view

Much of his work was first-hand accounts of the Mediterranean and North Africa. He quizzed merchants for information about India, which was the eastward extreme of the known world at that time. His map was not much of a departure from those used by Eratosthenes and others 200 years before. It showed Strabo's homeland, then known as Asia Minor, at the center of the world, with a single landmass surrounded by an ocean.

POMPONIUS MELA

A contemporary geographer of Strabo, only this time based in the far west of the Classical world, (modern Spain), Pomponius Mela divided the world into five climate zones, two of which were too cold or hot respectively for human habitation. Mela also asserted that beyond the desert region to his south, would lie more hospitable temperate areas inhabited by a southern population of humans, so far uncontacted by those in the north.

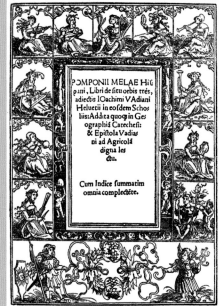

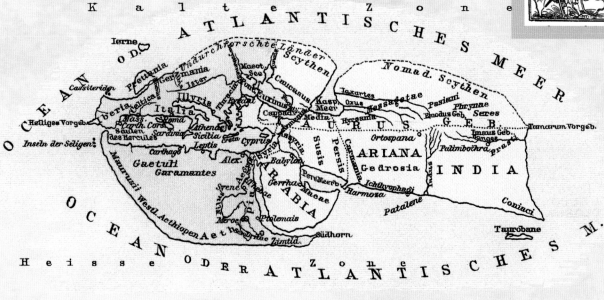

This 19th-century German rendering of Strabo's map of the world divides his landmass into three continents: Europe, Asia, and Libya (the Greek term for Africa). Such a division (largely arbitrary between Europe and Asia) persists to this day.

☐ Europa   ☐ Asia   ☐ Libya

9 The End of the World

THE PERIPATETIC SCHOOL OF ARISTOTLE CAST A LONG SHADOW ON THE EARTH SCIENCES THAT LASTED CENTURIES. However, ideas from its main philosophical rival, Stoicism, also had an impact on how future researchers interpreted evidence.

While the Peripatetic philosophers were named for walking around, the Stoics got their name from talking in the shade of a stoa, or colonnade. Aristotle's view was that changes in nature—be they weather upheavals or earthquakes and volcanoes—were part of a process that was leading toward a perfectly harmonious end state. So any catastrophic destruction would always be balanced by some process of rejuvenation. The Stoics disagreed. They reasoned that the planet would be destroyed in a catastrophe, which would remove evidence of the planet's past—and then a new version would emerge.

Myths of great floods, which wipe out entire civilizations, were evidence of the Stoics' assertion that the world was periodically destroyed and recreated.

10 Pliny's Natural History

IN 77 CE, PLINY THE ELDER, A ROMAN HISTORIAN, SAILOR, AND MAN OF LETTERS, PUBLISHED *NATURALIS HISTORIA*, which purported to contain everything there was to know about earth sciences to date.

Pliny's immense work contained 37 sections which covered subjects like astronomy, mathematics, and biology—even sculpture and painting—as well as looking at earth science in the fields of geography, mineralogy, and mining. He did not gather all this knowledge himself, but his goal was to present the work of others—always credited—in one text. He was able to build on works, updating information about minerals and mining from Theophrastus's *On Stones*, and the geography of Strabo. However, the earth science for which Pliny is best remembered is not included. Two years after publication, Pliny led a rescue mission by sea to save friends living close to Vesuvius, a volcano towering above the southwestern coast of Italy that had started erupting. But on the shore near the volcano, Pliny was overcome by toxic fumes and died.

The best record of the eruption of Vesuvius comes not from Pliny the Elder, but from his nephew, Pliny the Younger, who declined to join his uncle's foolhardy mission.

11 Source of Rain

IN ANCIENT CHINESE CONFUCIAN TEACHING, RAIN IS A GIFT FROM HEAVEN, A THEORY THAT WAS INTERPRETED LITERALLY. That is, until Wang Chong, a Han-Dynasty philosopher, formulated the first accurate water cycle theory.

Wang Chong's great work was the book *Lunheng* (Critical Essays), produced in 80 CE, which contained a wide body of thought from the natural sciences to literature and mythology. When it comes to meteorology, Wang Chong had little time for the traditional thinking. Indeed, rain does come from above, he admitted, but that did not mean that the water came from the same location as the stars.

Clouds of moisture

In Chinese legends, a Dragon King ruled each of the Four Seas: to the north, Lake Baikal in Siberia; the Yellow Sea in the east; in the south, the South China Sea; and to the west, Qinghai Lake in central China.

He lamented that the literal Confucian reasoning had led to most attempts at weather forecasting being linked to the motion of heavenly objects, such as the Moon, when the truth of the matter is plain to see. While ascending tall mountains to visit the many temples built high on the peaks, a traveler's clothes become wet (as they would during a rain shower) when they pass through the clouds that shroud the slopes. The simple explanation is that rain and clouds are fundamentally the same thing, Wang Chong explained. Clouds are in the sky, and that is why rain always falls downward—although not all the way from heaven. The moisture in the clouds comes from the forests "steaming," by which he means liquid water evaporating from the surface and rising up to form clouds at higher levels. Wang Chong used the Chinese concept of qi energy as the mechanism for this process, and it forms a good initial description of Earth's water cycle.

The temple on Mount Emei, one of the four sacred Buddhist mountains of China, stands above the clouds—and above the rain.

DRAGON KING

Chinese legend associates rainfall with the lóng, or flying dragon. In the myth of the Four Seas, the Chinese people are suffering a great drought, and the Dragon King who ruled the weather takes pity on them and sends four lóng to create great rainstorms. These storms created four mighty rivers: The Pearl, Yellow, Black and Lóng Rivers (the last one is better known as the Yangtze) which irrigate the farms of China to this day.

12 Maps of the World

CLAUDIUS PTOLEMY WAS A PROLIFIC SCIENCE WRITER FROM THE 2ND CENTURY CE, WHOSE WORK INFLUENCED GLOBAL THOUGHT FOR CENTURIES. His book *Geography* contained detailed maps of the known world and served as history's first atlas.

The illuminated title page of a 15th-century Latin translation of Ptolemy's Geography.

Ptolemy was of Greek descent but was a Roman citizen living in Egypt, which then was a wealthy Roman province. His works, most notably *Geography* and *Almagest*, a book about astronomy, were particularly influential because they formed a bridge between the philosophy of Classical Greece and the Golden Age of Islam from around the 12th century, when the seat of world learning shifted from the Library of Alexandria to Baghdad's House of Wisdom. There, the ideas crystallized in Ptolemy's work were further developed and then began to spread into Europe at the dawn of the Renaissance.

The known world

The original version of *Geography* was published around 80 CE, but that edition is now lost, and what we know about it comes from versions that have been copied, translated, and embellished innumerable times. Scholars have gathered 65 maps that were included in the book at some time or other. Most are regional maps showing rivers, mountains, and major settlements. Ptolemy created these works by copying or

Although still wildly distorted at the poles, the Armadillo projection gives near equal space to Earth's inhabited regions.

MAP PROJECTIONS

Ptolemy's world map used a novel projection to help display the spherical three-dimensional surface of Earth on a flat, two-dimensional surface. Mathematicians quickly showed that it is impossible to represent the landmasses of Earth accurately on the large scale without distortions somewhere. The question is where to distort? The Mercator project from the 16th century squashed equatorial regions and enlarged northern areas—including Europe and North America. This map is still widely used and gives a false impression as to the true size of countries in these regions.

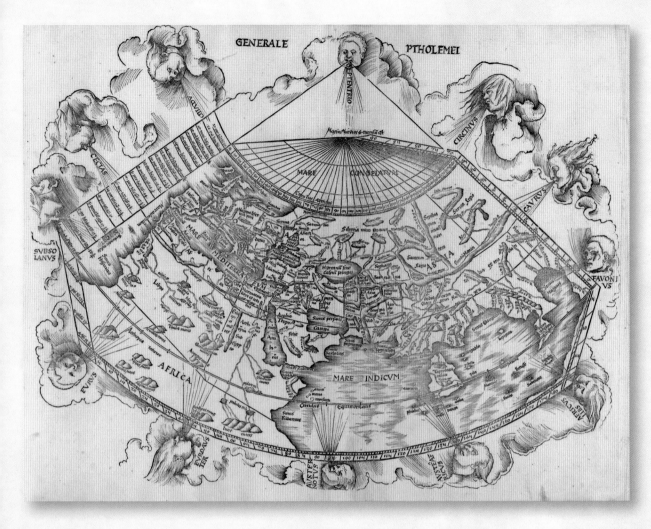

Ptolemy's world map projected the known landmasses onto a quarter circle. He knew the size of the planet and the approximate distances to the different continents, and so assumed there were still three-quarters of the world to discover. The first atlases that showed maps of a fully circular globe were published in 1570.

combining the maps of others and adding details from other sources. The regions close to the Mediterranean Sea were more accurately rendered than the far-flung regions like Britain, Ireland, and Sri Lanka, which would have been compiled from the reports of a few intrepid explorers.

The single world map was an updating of the one developed by Eratosthenes and Strabo. Ptolemy did not draw it himself, and it is generally credited to a cartographer called Agathodaemon of Alexandria. Unlike earlier maps, the ocean did not surround the known world on all sides. The eastern coast of Africa was extended as terra incognita (unknown land) which enclosed the Indian Ocean. The eastern end of the world had by now extended to the Malay Peninsula and the Gulf of Thailand.

Longitude and latitude

Ptolemy's world map was one of the first to use lines of longitude and latitude to help pinpoint locations. The lines of longitude spanned 180 degrees of the globe, so we are seeing the northeast quarter of the planet. The prime meridian, where longitude is 0, ran through the mythical Fortunate Isles off the coast of Africa (probably the Canaries). Lines of latitude, running east-west around the globe, were drawn north from the Equator (which was too far north). Again, the measurements were a bit out. The landmass shown actually stretches only about a third of the way around the globe.

IMAGO MUNDI

The oldest surviving "image" or map of the world (*imago mundi*) is a clay tablet from Babylon that dates back to the 6th century BCE. It would not have been much use in getting around. It shows the Euphrates River with Babylon and neighboring states along the banks. The whole region is surrounded by a ring of "bitter river" or ocean.

13 Cause of the Tides

THE RISE AND FALL OF THE SEA EACH DAY IS A SIGNIFICANT FORCE FOR COASTAL COMMUNITIES AND SAILORS. The process that drives this global phenomenon took many centuries to figure out.

The Venerable Bede was the most important historian in Dark-Age England.

The tide rises and falls twice every day—flowing and ebbing, in maritime terminology—and every two weeks tides fluctuate from a high-water spring tide to a lower neap tide. This pattern was linked to the motion and phases of the Moon in ancient times, but it was the English monk, the Venerable Bede, who in 725 set out a full description of how the two cycles worked in his book *The Reckoning of Time*. He saw that high tide was four-fifths of an hour later every day, the same time interval as the rise and set of the Moon. Every 59 days, the Moon rises and sets 57 times, and there are 114 tides (twice 57). He also noted that the strength and direction of the wind can have an effect on the height of the tide.

Bede was working during the Dark Ages, a period of European history when the historical record thins out following the fall of the Roman Empire in the 5th century. Bede is one of the few scholars whose work has survived from that time. Until the Renaissance, or rebirth of knowledge in Europe, began around the 14th century, the Islamic world was the center of world learning. Nevertheless, while many Arabian and Persian scholars continued to explore the link between tides and Moon, one of the most influential thinkers from this period, al-Kindi, offered a new theory in the 9th century. He proposed that the tides rose each day due to the expansion of water as it was heated by the Sun moving overhead. As the Sun moved away again, the water would cool and contract, and the tide would drop. (On a firmer footing, Al-Kindi said that wind was caused in the same way, as hot air expanded and rushed outward to cold areas.)

Bede lived in the kingdom of Northumbria in what is now northeast England, an area that was ruled for much its history from Bamburgh Castle which guards the tidal flats of the North Sea coast.

SPRING AND NEAP TIDES

Although the spring equinox and the vernal or autumnal one are both characterized by very high tides, the term "spring tide" relates to the notion that the water is leaping up the shore to a higher position. Neap is derived from an Old English word which means "weak." This tide is caused by the pull of the Moon's gravity, which creates a bulge several meters above sea level. The bulge moves around the globe as Earth rotates beneath it. A corresponding bulge forms on the opposite side of the planet. During a spring tide, the bulge is enlarged because the pull of the Moon is augmented by the pull of the Sun as well. During a neap tide, the pull of the Sun and Moon are perpendicular to one another.

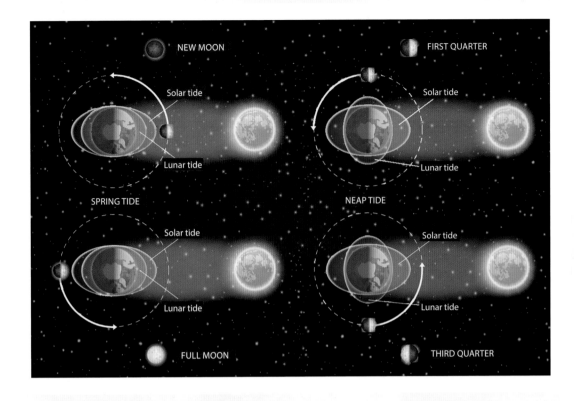

Enlightenment forces

In 1608, the Dutch mathematician Simon Stevin finally dismissed the notion that the tide was a weather phenomenon, and instead proposed that the Moon gave out a force that pulled the water up the shore. This was reinforced a year later by Johannes Kepler, who set out the laws governing orbits like that of the Moon. He thought the Moon might be a magnet of some kind. In 1687, Isaac Newton's law of gravity explained tides—as well as many other things—and by the 1770s, Pierre-Simon Laplace had developed equations for calculating tide times for a stretch of coast, but the math was fiendish. Another century passed before Lord Kelvin invented an analogue computer to do the sums, and these clockwork devices were still in use in the 1970s.

SIMON STEVIN

This Dutch mathematician's interest in tides was due in part to his invention of the land yacht, a wind-powered vehicle that "sailed" along beaches. However, his biggest contribution was to introduce decimal fractions in Europe, where numbers smaller than one were written in terms of tenths, hundredths, and so on.

14 Voyages to America

IN 1492, COLUMBUS SAILED THE OCEAN BLUE, BUT FORGET ABOUT ALL THAT FOR NOW. VIKINGS HAD BEEN EXPLORING THE GRAY WATERS OF THE NORTH ATLANTIC five centuries before. The hardy Norsemen even set up home in North America for a few decades. History could have been very different.

Leif Erikson's Vikings explored to the west of Greenland and found the coast of what is now Canada.

It is generally agreed that the ancestors of today's Native Americans walked there from Asia at least 14,000 years ago. Earth was in an ice age at that time, and the sea levels were much lower due to a great volume of ice covering the land. As a result, what is now the Bering Strait was dry land—a region called Beringia—connecting Siberia to Alaska. Beringia was covered by rising sea levels around 11,000 years ago, and from then on the Americas were only accessible by advanced seafarers.

It took another 10,000 years for such explorers to make the trip, this time arriving on the eastern coast of North America in the year 1002. The crew were Norse, also often called Vikings, who hailed originally from Scandinavia, but belonged to a community that had settled in Iceland in the 870s and more recently in Greenland.

Colonists from the Viking settlements in Greenland built a small village in what is now Newfoundland, but abandoned this new home within a generation.

PREDICTING AMERICA

Unaware that Viking explorers were already there, the Persian geographer al-Biruni predicted the existence of the Americas in 1037. Having calculated the size of Earth, he found that the known landmasses were bunched up on one side of the globe. To balance things out, he said, there must be more land on the other side of the world.

ПОЧТА СССР 1973
6к
Абу Рейхан Бируни
1000 лет со дня рождения

Ocean-going technology

Norse longships were tough, clinker-built vessels (with overlapping planks) that could withstand rough seas. They were powered by sail or oars and steered with a large paddle at the rear on the right, or starboard side (a term derived from "steer-board"). A longship's bow and stern were hard to distinguish because the ships were built to move equally easily in both directions, a design feature that came in handy when navigating rivers and narrow inlets. Legend has it that the Icelandic Norse used clear crystals as the "Viking compass." This stone, possibly a clear form of calcite, split the light that shone through it, and could be used to locate the Sun even when it was shrouded by clouds—and thus they could always orientate the ship.

Off course

Despite the ability to make long sea voyages, the Vikings discovered North America by accident. Leif Erikson, a Greenlander, was blown off course on a return trip from Norway, and came across a land filled with wild wheat and grapes. Naming it Vinland, meaning "farmland," he soon returned with a better equipped crew of Greenland Vikings to explore the region. They found frozen tundra (probably Baffin Island); dense forests (Labrador); and finally made it back to Vinland, where they established a small settlement. In the 1960s, archeologists found evidence of this first European foothold in America, at L'Anse aux Meadows on the northern tip of Newfoundland. The village, named Leifsbudir, did not last long. The Vikings fell out with the locals, who the Norse recorded as the *skraeling* (meaning "the people who wear animal skins").

15 Liquid Rock

THE PERSIAN SCHOLAR AVICENNA IS BEST REMEMBERED AS A PHYSICIAN AND PHILOSOPHER. HOWEVER, HE FOUND ROOM IN HIS BOOK *The Book of Healing* to discuss the earth sciences, including the source of new rock.

According to Avicenna's theory, lava contained a rock-forming liquid called succus lapidificatus.

Despite being called the *The Book of Healing*, readers in 1027 when it was published would find little mention of medical procedures. Avicenna (his real name was ibn Sina) suggested that rocks were formed by contact with a liquid. That would explain how stone fossils form from dead lifeforms. In addition, Avicenna pondered whether mountains are the result of sudden upheavals or slow processes that require a long time scale. Such thoughts would have been heretical in Europe at the time.

ERIK THE RED

As his name suggests, Leif Erikson was the son of an Erik—the Red—himself a Viking explorer who is credited with being the first European to settle Greenland. Icelandic sagas record that others had found it before Erik, but he made a success of founding a settlement there in 985. He named it Greenland to attract colonists—although climate differences did mean it was not quite as cold then as it is now. For 500 years, a community of about 2,500 Norse lived on the south-western coast, but abandoned their homes when the climate grew colder in the late 1400s.

16 Making Dry Land

THE CHINESE SCIENTIST SHEN KUO WAS NOT THE FIRST TO WONDER WHY SEASHELL FOSSILS were found in high mountain rocks, but in the 1070s he linked that and other data to propose a process of how land formed.

Marine fossils in mountains far inland is obvious proof that there used to be a seabed there. Shen Kuo agreed, and proposed that layers of silt had built up on the seabed over a long period, making the rock rise up above the water's surface to make a landmass. Fossil bamboo in deserts too dry for it to grow showed Shen Kuo that land could change as well. For example, forces beneath the surface could push it into mountains. The mountain rock was then eroded, washing away as silt and other sediments that traveled along rivers to the sea, where it made a fresh layer on the seabed. All that was needed was a lot of time.

Fossils in the soft rocks of the Taihang Mountains in central China were the starting point for Shen Kuo's theory of geomorphology.

17 Rainbow Science

THE ETHEREAL SPREAD OF A RAINBOW'S COLORS has long attracted attention from scientists. In 1300, glass spheres helped throw light on the subject.

Seneca the Younger, a Roman philosopher from the 1st century CE, was the first to make headway with an explanation for the rainbow. He noticed that the phenomenon always appears in the sky opposite the Sun. He also noted that the same effect could be made with a splash or spray of water. His conclusion was that the rainbow was a reflection off a mirror-like surface created by the droplets of water. This became the accepted view—held even by al-Haytham, the Arabian founder of optics, the science of light, in the 11th century. However, the truth was not revealed until 1300, when German monk

Theodoric's diagrams of his rainbow discovery had to be drawn in black and white.

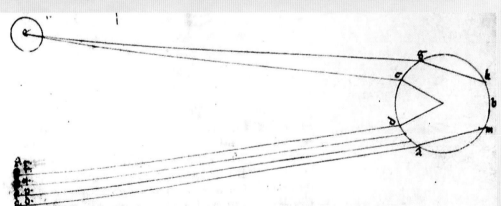

Theodoric of Freiberg recreated raindrops out of glass globes filled with water. He saw that a light beam shining into the globe was redirected, or refracted, onto the back of the "raindrop," where it was reflected out again. A second refraction occurred as the light left the droplet, transitioning back into the air, which split the white light into its many colors. The rainbow we see is the result of these refractions and reflections. It is actually a halo but we can only really see the semicircle against the sky.

18 Treasure Voyages

In 1405, the Chinese Ming emperor ordered an expedition of exploration like no one had ever seen before. Giant ships set sail to explore the oceans—and promote the greatness of China.

Zhang He is venerated across large regions of Southeast Asia as a figure who spread both Islam and Chinese influence.

THE COMPASS

The treasure fleet used magnetic compasses for navigation, a technology that had recently spread to the West. However, for most of the first millennium the Chinese used the compass in rituals to track the flow of spirits through a landscape. This was done with a spoon-shaped lodestone (natural magnet) that was designed to point south (below). European sailors decided that north was a more significant direction.

The Ming Dynasty wanted to broaden their view of the world, and to change the way foreigners saw China. On a total of seven voyages, a vast fleet led by Admiral Zhang toured the Indian Ocean, visiting East Africa, Arabia, India, and the western islands of what is now Indonesia. The voyages were chiefly trade and diplomatic missions that gave neighboring states no illusions as to the might of imperial China, but they also enhanced Chinese knowledge of the Indian Ocean region.

Zhang He largely followed coastal trading routes, but also discovered new sea routes and exchanges of goods and ideas. However, the treasure fleet program was ended in 1433, and that left a naval power vacuum in the Indian Ocean, which was filled in the later half of the century and into the 1500s by European explorers who came eastward around the southern tip of Africa. If the Chinese voyages had continued, world history might have been very different.

Zhang He's treasure fleet contained enormous ships that were at least twice as large as vessels built anywhere else at the time (although the exact dimensions are disputed). Reports of the fleets are also hard to verify, but accounts suggest that voyages included more than 40 large treasure ships—which were meant to project Chinese wealth, not to plunder other nations—plus another 200 ships, and a combined personnel of 28,000 people.

19 Magnetic Navigation

FOR MUCH OF HUMAN HISTORY, SEA CAPTAINS WERE GENERALLY LOATHE TO STRAY OUT OF SIGHT OF LANDMARKS along the shore lest they get lost. The magnetic compass changed that, and offered new navigation techniques.

HENRY THE NAVIGATOR

Prince Henry of Portugal ruled a nation on the far western edge of the world, far from the trading hubs of Europe and Asia. What his nation did have, however, was access to the ocean, and perhaps that was a route to the rest of the world that Portugal could control. In around 1418 Henry asked sailors, mathematicians, and engineers to create technology needed for long voyages. The Age of Exploration had begun.

Lodestones, naturally magnetic pieces of iron ore, were used as compasses in China as far back as 200 BCE. By the 1300s CE, compass technology had spread through Asia to Europe, and it was here—specifically in Spain and Portugal—that open-water navigation far from land was pioneered in the 1400s. The compass was a crucial tool in this endeavor, as it reliably always points in the same direction—north. However, Atlantic explorers began to realize that the north indicated by the magnet could shift position—or at least appear to shift. These changes are now called magnetic declination, the angular difference between true north located at the North Pole and Magnetic North, which is a few degrees over beneath the Canadian Arctic. The exact declination depends on the location east and west of the Magnetic North, and medieval navigators used it as a crude means of estimating longitude as they crossed the empty ocean.

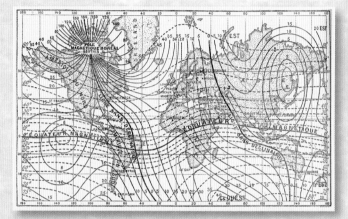

A 19th-century map shows the rough directions to Magnetic North from different locations (although heavily distorted by the projection.)

20 Weather Measurements

DURING THE RENAISSANCE SCIENTISTS BEGAN TO USE DATA AND RECORD FACTS. When it came to the studying the weather, that process was begun by an archetypal Renaissance Man.

Leon Battista Alberti dabbled in a bit of everything—poetry, architecture, mathematics, and code-breaking. Plus, he invented the anemometer, a device for measuring the speed of the wind. His design from the 1450s would be easily recognizable today because it has remained largely unchanged ever since. It involved vanes or blades radiating from a central axle. Wind from any

MAXIMUM AND MINUMUM

In 1780, James Six invented a U-shaped thermometer that had steel markers on top of the mercury. The left marker dropped as the temperature fell and stayed put at the lowest temperature. The right marker rose to the highest temperature that day.

direction would catch a vane and push the axle around—moving the next vane along into the path of wind. The result was a device that spun around, and the number of rotations per minute would indicate the wind's strength.

The anemometer was later improved by using cups instead of vanes; their curvature helped the device to spin evenly. Such devices are seen today on weather stations, such as at airports and docks. Propeller-shaped wind gauges rotate around a horizontal axis like a mini windmill. This version also swings to face the wind, so gives direction as well as speed.

THE RAIN GAUGE

Around the same time as Alberti's contribution to weather measurements, another was being made on the far side of the known world, in Korea. The 1400s was the heyday of the Josean Dynasty of Korea, and the king ordered that a standard rain gauge—the cheugugi—be installed in numbers across the land to collect information about rainfall in different agricultural zones. Only one cheugugi survives (right). It is a steel cylinder about 32 cm (12.6 in) deep that is held firm on a sturdy stone base.

Getting steamy?

The humidity in the air is a good indicator of the chance of rain. Ancient Chinese weather forecasters used the weight of lumps of charcoal as a humidity measurer, or hygrometer—the lumps would get heavier as they absorbed moisture from the air. In the mid 1400s, a contemporary of Alberti called Nicholas of Cusa invented a hygrometer based around a long human hair. Hair gets longer when damp (and contracts when dry), and these changes were made apparent by the way the hygrometer held the hair under a gentle tension. The hair hygrometer design is sometimes attributed to the artist, engineer, and all-round genius Leonardo da Vinci, who included a drawing of it in his *Codex Atlanticus* sketchbook in 1480.

The Tower of Winds in the agora, or marketplace, of ancient Athens is considered the world's first weather station. As well as a wind vane on the roof to show wind direction, the tower had a sundial and a water clock to keep time for the citizens of the city.

21 Voyage of Columbus

CHRISTOPHER COLUMBUS IS THE MOST FAMOUS EXPLORER IN HISTORY. HE WAS THE FIRST SEA CAPTAIN to return to Europe with firm reports of a New World on the western shore of the Atlantic. And it was all thanks to a big mistake.

FIRST HURRICANE

Columbus returned to the Caribbean in 1493, planning to get rich by creating a slave industry. The Caribbean is the world's most active hurricane zone, and Columbus was forced to shelter his fleet at the southern tip of Hispaniola from one such storm. His report of what he described as a "sea monster" was the first account of a hurricane to reach Europe. The word "hurricane" comes from the language of the Taíno people, who occupied the Caribbean islands before the arrival of Columbus—and were effectively wiped out by the ensuing settlements set up by Columbus and other colonialists.

The history of the Americas turns on the date of October 12, 1492. This was when Columbus's fleet landed on an island in the Bahamas, and as a result, the kingdoms of Europe turned their attention westward. The history of the American continents from before that day are described as Pre-Columbian, and within months of the news of the New World reaching Europe, adventurers and settlers began to arrive to take claim of a piece of the territory—and the rest is world history.

Ocean blue

It is certainly ironic, but not unsurprising that such a huge moment in history resulted from a serious miscalculation. The story of Columbus has been folded into the foundation myths of today's American nations, and the facts are hard to follow. However, the general story goes that Columbus, an Italian seaman, had a plan to find a westerly route to the Indies—most notably, the Spice Islands in what we would now call Indonesia. The go-to guy for funding was the King of Portugal, but his navigation experts

Columbus prepares for departure from Palos on the southern Spanish coast. Despite what legend says, his crew were unconcerned about falling off a flat Earth, but were worried they lacked the resources to make it to Asia by sea.

A ROUTE TO INDIA

Columbus's attempt to interest Portugal in his voyage were hampered by news that Bartolomeu Dias had recently found the southern tip of Africa, making Asia accessible by an eastward route. Dias's name for the African landmark, Cape of Storms, was switched to Cape of Good Hope to boost its public appeal. In 1497, Vasco de Gama led a Portuguese expedition on this route and arrived in India (for real this time) a year later. The outward route to India caught winds that took ships southwest right up close to what is now the coast of Brazil—a territory that soon became a Portuguese colony.

rejected it out of hand. Columbus did eventually get the ships he needed from the Spanish royals, who also thought he was a bit crazy but liked the idea of beating the Portuguese to any possible reward—no matter how remote. (As a testament to their low expectations, the Spanish allowed Columbus to make himself viceroy—a proxy king—of any land he discovered.)

Columbus's crew were also none too keen because, as re-tellings inform us, they were afraid of falling off the edge of the world.

Halfway around

After four weeks at sea sailing west from the Canary Islands (at the time one of most westerly known bits of dry land), the story goes that the crew begged to be allowed to return home. Columbus calmed their fears by asking for three more days—and as luck would have it land was spotted in the nick of time. Columbus thought he was in the Indies of eastern Asia, and because of this, Native Americans were known as Indians for the best part of the next 500 years.

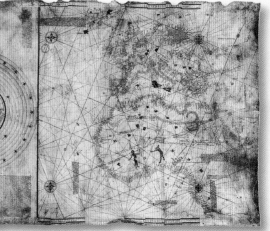

This map, dating from 1490, is on show in Lisbon, Portugal. It is thought to be the version used by Columbus on his famous first voyage to America.

This error was built on a bigger one that underwrote the whole enterprise. Columbus felt sure he could sail from Spain to Asia in five weeks or so because he had made several errors in calculating the size of the planet and the size of the continents. Working with measurements from Greek and Arabic sources, he muddled his units and ended up with a planet that was 25 percent smaller than previous estimates. Secondly, he thought that the Far East was much closer to Europe, stretching the land around the planet so the distance he thought he needed to sail was less than half of the true value. This was the real reason that his plan was rebuffed by the Portuguese navigators, and why his crew were unsettled after weeks at sea. They feared starving before their fleet made it all the way around, and were only saved by stumbling into what became known as America.

22 Circumnavigation

DESPITE THE UNEXPECTED SUCCESS OF COLUMBUS'S VOYAGE, the King of Spain, who had sponsored the venture, was still left without a westward route to Asia. In 1519, another fleet set out in search of one.

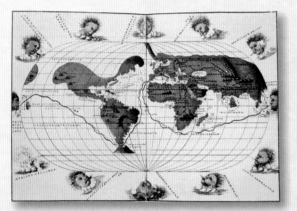

The route of Magellan's fateful voyage around the world, which took nearly three years.

Magellan's voyage of discovery was cut short after he became embroiled in a tribal war in what is now the Philippines. He was an early casualty in the fighting.

In 1494, when the true scope of ocean exploration—and the trade that could flow from it—was now clear, the two leading maritime powers, Spain and Portugal, agreed to divide the world in half. Their Treaty of Tordesillas said that anything west of a line drawn down the middle of the Atlantic would be Spanish, and Portugal would control whatever was to the east. It turned out that the coast of Brazil was east of the line, which gave Portugal an American foothold.

A new ocean

The commander of the Spanish fleet that set out to Asia was a Portuguese navigator called Ferdinand Magellan. He led five ships across the Atlantic Ocean, along the Brazilian coast and around the southern tip of South America (see box). There Magellan's expedition became only the second group of Europeans to sail west of the Americas. (A few years earlier, a Spanish explorer had crossed the Isthmus of Panama to reach the west coast.) Magellan named the ocean the "peaceful sea," a term that has come down to us as the name Pacific. It took more than three months to cross this, the largest ocean on Earth. (Its area is about the same as that of all other oceans combined.) Eighteen months into the voyage, the fleet was within striking distance of the Spice Islands, and stopped at Cebu, now in the Philippines. Magellan became embroiled in a local war and died in a skirmish. It fell upon Juan Sebastián Elcano to bring the fleet around Africa and back to Spain. They had been away just shy of three years. Of the 270 crew who set out, 18 returned.

CAPE HORN

The southern tip of South America is called Cape Horn. It has a complex coastline of inlets, islands, and bays, which Magellan named Tierra del Fuego (Land of Fire) because the European fleet could see many fires along the shore at night, lit by local people to keep warm—or perhaps prepare for attack. Magellan chose to enter a deep inlet with salty water which lead through from the Atlantic to the Pacific. The seaway is called the Strait of Magellan today.

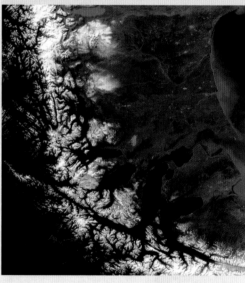

23 The Nature of Metals

DURING THE DARK AGES, INVESTIGATION OF ROCKS, MINERALS, AND ESPECIALLY METALS HAD BEEN DOMINATED BY WIZARDLY ALCHEMISTS. In 1556, a German doctor took a more clear-eyed approach.

The central goal of alchemy was to uncover the magic that underwrote what we would now understand as chemical reactions. Your average alchemist was interested in getting rich quickly, by creating gold from lead and discovering the elixir of life. Their work was ultimately fruitless but it did begin a catalog of useful substances, especially different kinds of metal. In 1556, Georg Pawer, a physician from a mining town in what is now the Czech Republic, published a compendium of mineralogy, called *De re metallica* (The Nature of Metals). He chose the nom de plume of Agricola (meaning "farmer" in Latin, as "pawer" does in some parts of Germany). The book outlined how to recognize ores, where to find deposits, and the latest technology of mining and smelting as it stood in the 16th century. Agricola's was not the only technology manual of the era, but it proved the most significant, with copies still in use 200 years later.

Agricola's book was filled with practical guidance—complete with illustrations—on how to find and extract minerals.

24 The Submarine

EXPLORATION OF THE DEEP OCEANS BEGAN WITH THE DIVING BELL. IN 1578, BRITISH MATHEMATICIAN William Bourne put forward the idea of a boat that could be rowed underwater. Now there was a challenge!

Bourne's design was a vessel built of waterproof leather on a wooden frame and would be submerged by using hand ratchets to pull in the sides, thus reducing its volume.

Bourne never built his boat, and so the credit for the first actual submarine goes to Cornelius van Drebbel, a Dutch inventor. Drebbel's submarine was similar to that proposed by Bourne, with an outer hull of greased leather over a wooden frame. Oars, extending out through tight-fitting leather flaps, provided the means of propulsion. In 1620 Drebbel successfully steered his craft 4 to 5 meters (13 to 16 feet) beneath the waters of the River Thames in London, England. From then on submarine technology was developed for warfare and it was not until 1960 that deep-sea vessels were developed for exploration.

This illustration of the submerged Drebbel submarine was rather wishful thinking. The Thames flowing through London would never be clear enough to see a vessel under the water—especially not in the 1600s, in the days before sewers.

25 Air Pressure

"NATURE ABHORS A VACUUM" IS A CONCEPT DATING BACK TO ARISTOTLE AND CLASSICAL GREECE. But investigations into whether a vacuum was possible or not would lead to a new understanding of the nature of the atmosphere, and provide a crucial factor in predicting the weather.

Like so many scientific stories from the 17th century, this one begins with Galileo Galilei, already famed for his discoveries about the form and behavior of the Solar System. At the height of his powers in 1630, Galileo was asked to explain why water siphons could not lift water over a particularly large hill. The reasoning at the time was that a pump would draw water through a siphon by creating at least the possibility of a vacuum. The water would rush in to fill the space, obeying Aristotle's pithy aphorism, and moving through the pipe as it did so. Galileo's suggestion was that even the power of a vacuum had its limit. After Galileo had died, his assistant Evangelista Torricelli returned to the siphon problem and studied it in miniature, scaled down ten times. He closed one end of a glass tube and filled it with mercury—a liquid that is 14 times as dense as water. He then placed the open end of the tube into a bowl of mercury. The mercury in the tube always fell to 76 cm (30 inches). It appeared that a column of mercury had a maximum height too, and this was approximately 14 times smaller than

Using Torricelli's mercury tube to prove the existence of air pressure had far-reaching consequences, not just for meteorology but also for the more fundamental sciences like physics and chemistry.

PERPETUAL MOTION MACHINE

Cornelius van Drebbel made a living by exciting the royalty of Europe with his inventions. As well as the submarine, he presented the perpetuum mobile, or so-called perpetual motion machine. It was really just an elaborate, tubular glass ring open at one end with an air bubble trapped by water at the closed end. With much showmanship, Drebbel showed off how the water shifted continuously in the tube. He said it was down to tidal forces and astrology—he would often vary explanations to suit particular audiences. William Shakespeare is said to have been inspired by the device to create the character Ariel, an enslaved spirit ruled by the wizard Prospero, in his 1611 play *The Tempest*. In fact, Drebbel's device relied simply on natural changes in the temperature and pressure of air around the water, which pushed the water back and forth. Less elaborate J-shaped versions were a curiosity in scientific circles at the time, and were a stepping stone to thermometer technology (see page 38).

that of a water column that marked the limit of the siphon. This was enough evidence for Torricelli to turn the theory of pumps and vacuums on its head. He found that a liquid was not raised by the pull of a vacuum but pushed by the weight of the air. A column reached its maximum height when its weight was balanced with that of the air. This earned Torricelli the rights to the invention of the barometer—a device for measuring air pressure—although others had tinkered with them before.

Torricelli's mercury tube became essential equipment for a new breed of Enlightenment scientists, and the glassworking technology behind it was repurposed 50 years later to make the first accurate thermometers.

Ups and downs

With Torricelli sent to an early grave by typhoid in 1647, Frenchman Blaise Pascal took over the investigation the following year. He sent his brother-in-law Florin Périer to Clermont-Ferrand at the foot of Puy de Dôme, a 1,460-m (4,790 ft) tall extinct volcano. Périer set up a mercury barometer in the town—where its level remained stable all day—and took another identical device with him up the mountain. Périer made meticulous measurements of the tube as he climbed, and at every stop, he found that the level of the mercury was dropping as he climbed higher and higher. This was as Pascal had predicted: the air pressure—or weight of the air—dropped with altitude as there was less air pushing down from above. Air pressure was also seen to fluctuate up and down from hour to hour and minute to minute, down at sea level. Falling mercury levels were soon linked to periods of unsettled rainy weather, while high pressure became a predictor of calm weather. But at the time, no one knew how that worked.

26 Weather Reports

IT IS A SELF-EVIDENT FACT THAT WEATHER CHANGES DO NOT SUDDENLY APPEAR; THERE ARE PLENTY OF SIGNS HERALDING THEIR ARRIVAL. If these signs could be observed over a wide area, predictions of the weather would improve. In 1654, an Italian duke and hobby scientist set up such a system.

Ferdinando II was an avid sponsor of the new sciences being developed in Renaissance Italy.

Ferdinando II de' Medici was the Grand Duke of Tuscany and lived most in the Pitti Palace, a lavish edifice in the heart of Florence. Florence was an epicenter of the Renaissance, and as a keen amateur alchemist, Ferdinando was in regular contact with the great artists, engineers, and new breed of scientists, such as Galileo. He was intrigud by all the new gadgets and gizmos being invented, such as the hygrometer (a humidity gauge), anemometer (for measuring wind speed), barometer (for air pressure), and thermoscope, which was a crude forerunner to the thermometer. Ferdinando is also reported to have invented the Galilean thermometer (inspired by the teachings of Galileo), which uses glass bulbs filled with alcohol at a variety of specific pressures. These bulbs floated in a column of water and rose and sank as the variations in temperature altered their density. It looked pretty but was unwieldy to use.

THE FIRST WEATHERMAN

The Medicis are credited with the first weather observations service, but the first weatherman—who collected systematic meteorological records—was William Merle. Merle worked in the early 1300s in Oxford, England. He kept a daily record of weather for the best part of 15 years, which is the oldest surviving data of its kind.

LONG-DISTANCE DATA

Despite its eventual failure, the Medici's example led to the development of weather observation networks elsewhere. Another leap forward came in 1849 when the Smithsonian Institution in Washington, D.C. began using the telegraph to collate weather data. The Institution had been founded in 1846, and its first chief was Joseph Henry (right), a pioneer of electromagnetic technology and one of the inventors of the telegraph. Observations made everyday at the 150 stations across the nation were used to create a Daily Weather Map displayed for public view at the Smithsonian Institution Building or "The Castle" on the National Mall.

On trial

As one of the richest men in the world (although the Medici fortune was beginning to wane), Ferdinando sent sets of his measuring devices to locations across Italy and beyond into what is now Austria, France, and Poland, creating the world's first weather stations. Data from these locations—ten in all—was sent back to Florence for analysis at the Accademia del Cimento. Set up by Ferdinando's brother Leopoldo, this roughly translates as the Academy of Trials (or, better still, "of Experiments"). It was almost another world first—a scientific institute—but the Medicis ran it as a club, and eventually got distracted by other things. Few of the weather records survive, and none of the conclusions drawn from them.

27 Rock Strata

IN 1669, THE DANE NIELS STEENSEN, ALSO KNOWN BY A LATIN FORM NICOLAS STENO, LAID THE FOUNDATIONS of modern geology by describing the four rules that govern how rocks form in layers.

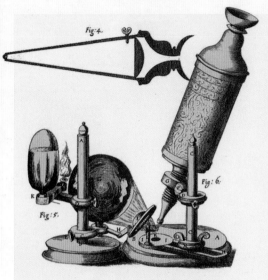

CLOSE-UP LOOK

Robert Hooke was the first person to examine fossils under a microscope, publishing his findings in 1665 in a book called *Micrographia*. The microscope was a very new instrument in those days, and through it Hooke saw similarities between the structures of petrified wood and living wood. He suggested that the organic material turned to stone if it was immersed in water that was rich in dissolved minerals.

Steno's interest in the history of Earth and its rocks was piqued by his work on fossils (see box below). A few years later he created an overarching theory of stratigraphy, the science that is concerned with strata, or layers of rock—which are evident in any canyon or other highly eroded landscape. He presented the theory in his 1669 essay *De solido intra solidum naturaliter contento* (Concerning a Solid Body Enclosed by Process of Nature Within a Solid). This work contained the principles that came to underwrite the field of physical geology, which concerns the rocks, minerals, and large-scale features of the planet.

Steno was a versatile researcher. As well as pondering the big-picture process of rock layering and the fossils within them, he was also interested in the fine structure of the crystals that made up the rocks.

Four rules

Steno's first rule was the Law of Superposition: "At the time when a given stratum was being formed, there was beneath it another substance which prevented the further descent of the comminuted [fragmented] matter …" Next came the Principle of Original

Horizontality: "At the time when one of the upper strata was being formed, the lower stratum had already gained the consistency of a solid." Third was the Principle of Lateral Continuity: "At the time when any given stratum was being formed it was either encompassed on its sides by another solid substance, or it covered the entire spherical surface of the Earth. Hence it follows that in whatever place the bared sides of the strata are seen, either a continuation of the same strata must be sought, or another solid substance must be found." Finally, Steno set out the Principle of Cross-Cutting Relationships: "At the time when any given stratum was being formed, all the matter resting upon it was fluid, and none of the upper strata [seen today] existed."

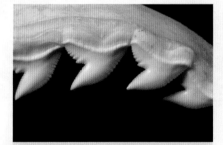

TONGUE STONES

In 1666, Steno was given a shark to dissect. As he did so, he was taken by the resemblance of the shark's teeth to triangular pieces of rock called tongue stones. Steno declared that the tongue stones were indeed the teeth of once-living sharks and argued that the original shark tissue had been gradually replaced over time by minerals. In other words, fossils were snapshots of life from different periods in history.

28 Temperature

HUMIDITY, WIND DETAILS, AND AIR PRESSURE READINGS WERE ALL VERY WELL, BUT WEATHER DATA HAS ANOTHER significant factor: the temperature. The road to a reliable thermometer proved a long one.

There had been many attempts to quantify the "temper" of the air, but the difficulty was creating something that could be made in large numbers with each device calibrated the same way. This means that wherever or whenever they were used, they would give a verifiable value that could be compared with a reading at another place or time. Temperature scales require only lower and upper points, with equal divisions, or degrees, between them. The first attempts at measuring temperature used thermoscopes (see box) but they proved useless. Tubes filled with colored alcohol worked well but were inconsistent. What was needed was an improvement in technology—and a more rigorous method of calibration.

Sick bed project

In 1702, the Danish astronomer Ole Rømer was stuck in bed with a broken leg, and decided to build an improved thermometer, the first one to properly fit the bill. He first found a glass tube that had a constant diameter, checking this by letting a drop of mercury fall through it and watching to see that it maintained a steady width. He fused the tube to a small globe which acted as a reservoir, then filled it with alcohol dyed yellow with saffron. His plan was for the spirit to rise by the same length as the width of the reservoir for every rise of 10 degrees on his scale.

Rømer's method for this is unclear. (In those days, thermometer-makers kept their skills secret so only they could make and sell devices of the correct quality.) He is thought to have marked the freezing temperature of water on the tube and added another mark to indicate the boiling point of water. He then divided the tube into eight sections, starting at the upper mark and making the seventh one at the lower point, and so the eighth appeared below this one. He gave the upper point a value of 60, and that meant the freezing point of water was 7.5°Rø. The 0°Rø represented the freezing point of a mixture of water and salts. Rømer made more thermometers based on this scale, with various designs for recording the temperature of air, water, and the body. Then a young German instrument maker came to visit in 1708.

Handwritten notes made by Daniel Fahrenheit in 1736 include a sketch for the shape of a mercury bulb.

THERMOSCOPE

On close inspection, a thermoscope varied little from Drebbel's perpetuum mobile of the early 1600s (see box, page 35). They used the expansion and contraction of air trapped in a glass bulb atop a tube to indicate the rise and fall of the temperature. Unlike a thermometer, the liquid (generally water) rising up the glass tube showed a fall in temperature, which was making the air bubble shrink. A warmer temperature made the air expand, and the water level drop. Some thermoscopes had gradations, or degrees, marked on them but none were suitable for creating a scale that could be replicated on another device.

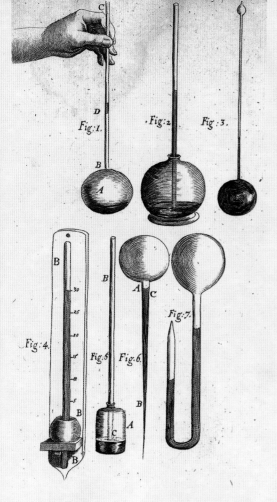

The 17th-century Irish scientist Robert Boyle, an early investigator of cold, used a variety of thermoscopes and thermometers but was unable to measure it in a verifiable way.

The Fahrenheit scale

The visitor was Daniel Fahrenheit, barely into his twenties. He went on to use Rømer's scale as inspiration for his own—which has stood the test of time somewhat better. It took Fahrenheit another 16 years to perfect his scale and his thermometer design.

The important difference was Fahrenheit's skill as a glassblower, which allowed him to construct the first functional mercury thermometers in 1714. By 1724 he had reorganized Rømer's gradations, removing the unhelpful half-degree points, and set three fixed points on the scale to aid with calibration. The zero point was the temperature of a mixture of ice, water, and a salt (which was a combination of sal ammoniac [ammonium chloride] and sea salt). The "frigorific" mixture was the coldest he could consistently produce, but he nevertheless did most of this low temperature work in winter to avoid the ice melting too fast.

The second point was the freezing point of water, set at 32 degrees Fahrenheit, roughly four times that of the Rømer degree. The third point was the temperature of the mouth, which was 96 degrees—slightly below regular body temperature. That meant that the upper mark at the boiling point of water was set at 212°F.

Fahrenheit struggled to market his effective but expensive product, and he died in poverty in 1736. It is thought he guarded his intellectual property so tightly that customers didn't know its advantages. Within a decade, the scientific community had made the Fahrenheit scale the standard, but by the 20th century it was replaced by the decimalized Celsius scale across the world (with the exception of the United States, of course).

THE SPEED OF LIGHT

The temperature scale was something of an afterthought for Ole Rømer. He had already found his place in history by measuring the speed of light. In 1676, while working in the Paris Observatory (pictured), he took an interest in Io, one of the four large moons of Jupiter discovered by Galileo in 1609. Rømer compared his observations of the moon with its orbital path as predicted by Kepler's laws. Io is hidden from Earth when it moves behind Jupiter, but Rømer knew the exact time it would reappear. However, he found that the moon always appeared around 10 minutes late, and realized that the light from the moon was not arriving instantaneously. There was a timelag as the light beamed to Earth and down his telescope. The delays got slightly longer as Earth moved away from Jupiter in its orbit around the Sun, and Rømer used this difference to calculate that light traveled at 220,000 km (136,702 miles) per second. This was 25 percent slower than the actual value measured today. Earlier researchers had tried to measure light speed with lamps and other equipment, but Rømer's was the first measurement attempt that resulted in an actual answer.

29 The Winds

THE SUCCESSFUL VOYAGES OF THE AGE OF EXPLORATION WERE MADE BY NAVIGATORS WHO made use of the prevailing winds that blew across the oceans. In 1735 a lawyer (of all people) explained why it was that the winds took on such a pattern.

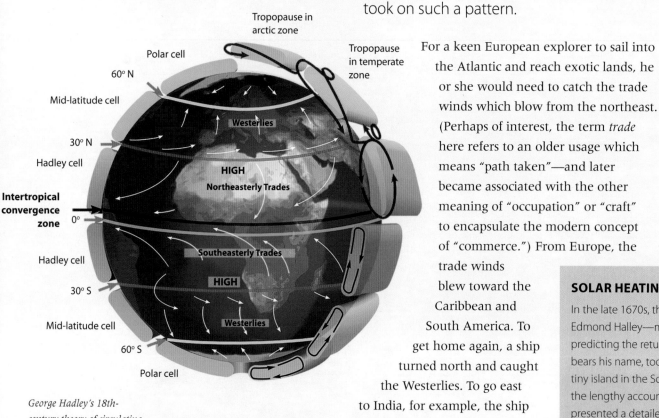

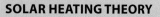

George Hadley's 18th-century theory of circulating cells of air is still the one used to describe the pattern of global winds.

For a keen European explorer to sail into the Atlantic and reach exotic lands, he or she would need to catch the trade winds which blow from the northeast. (Perhaps of interest, the term *trade* here refers to an older usage which means "path taken"—and later became associated with the other meaning of "occupation" or "craft" to encapsulate the modern concept of "commerce.") From Europe, the trade winds blew toward the Caribbean and South America. To get home again, a ship turned north and caught the Westerlies. To go east to India, for example, the ship first had to sail southwest almost to Brazil on the trade winds, then cross the Equator and catch westerlies around the Cape of Good Hope to enter the Indian Ocean. Navigators learned to be wary of tropical seas (around 30° from the Equator), where the winds

SOLAR HEATING THEORY

In the late 1670s, the English scientist Edmond Halley—most famous for predicting the return of the comet that bears his name, took a trip to St Helena, a tiny island in the South Atlantic. Among the lengthy accounts of his voyage, Halley presented a detailed map of the trade winds (pictured) and a theory about the origin of the wind. This said that the heat of the Sun is the ultimate source of the motion of the air. In summary, he suggested that warmer air rose up into the atmosphere and spread out, thus creating the winds. The westward swing of the trade winds was due, Halley said, to apparent the motion of the Sun across the sky. This notion is similar to the ideas of ancient China, that so exasperated Wang Chong 1600 years before (see page 19)—and Halley's theory was also found wanting.

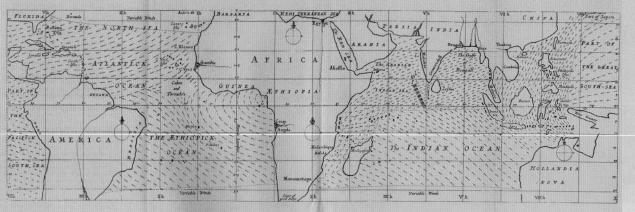

CORIOLIS EFFECT

Why don't winds blow directly north to south or vice versa? Why do the prevailing winds swing off course? George Hadley recognized that this was due to the rotation of Earth from west to east, but he was unable to explain the mechanism fully. This was achieved 100 years later by the French mathematician Gustave-Gaspard Coriolis. The Coriolis effect is seen on the surface of rotating spheres. Winds (or any moving objects) moving in a straight line trace a curved arc across the surface. North of the Equator, the winds swing to their right, so the south-flowing trade winds are deflected toward the southwest, while north-flowing winds swing east (and become westerly winds). South of the Equator, the deflection is to the winds' left. Theoretically the effect makes whirlpools—and water flowing down plug holes—turn in opposite directions in the north (clockwise) to the south (counterclockwise). Travelers between hemispheres often check this and are often disappointed. Even the slightest eddy in the water from a splash or drip will supersede the effect of Earth's rotation.

often died away, meaning a ship could float aimlessly. These regions were known as the Horse Latitudes, possibly because horses were the first cargo to jettison when supplies of freshwater ran low when becalmed (although there are other explanations offered).

Circulating air

Several earth scientists offered explanations for why the winds formed this pattern, most notably Edmond Halley (see box, left). Fifty years later, a full-time lawyer and amateur meteorologist called George Hadley did not accept Halley's version. Instead, he imagined the trade winds as the lowest portion of a vast circulation of air. He argued that the Sun's heat at the Equator made warm air rise and spread northward several miles above the surface. Once at the tropics, this air cooled and sank to the surface, where it was then circulated back to the Equator as wind. This circulation of air is now called a Hadley cell. There are two, one north of the Equator, the other south of the Equator, running right around the globe.

Similar cells form next to the Hadley cell, only this time the surface winds blow toward the poles—and swing off course due to Earth's rotation (see box, above) which is why they become westerlies. In polar regions yet another kind of cell produces weaker (but very cold) easterly winds.

Clipper ships were the pinnacle of sailing technology in the 19th century. Even when steel ships powered by engines were being developed, long-distance voyages to India and Australia were still best made by these lean ships designed to catch the strong southern westerlies.

30 The Shape of Earth

THE SCIENCE OF MEASURING THE SHAPE AND SIZE OF EARTH IS CALLED GEODESY. By the 18th century it was becoming apparent that our planet is not a perfect sphere.

CELSIUS SCALE

The Celsius scale has largely replaced Fahrenheit due to its simpler construction: 0°C is the freezing point of water, and 100°C is the boiling point. The Swede Anders Celsius, whose name is on the scale, was not the first person to have this idea, but he developed his version in 1742 a few years after taking part in the geodesic mission to frozen Lapland. His scale was initially focused on cold, so 100° was set at freezing point and 0° was boiling. Soon after Celsius's early death, Carl Linnaeus, who became a famous biologist, flipped the figures so 0° was cold and 100° hot. Despite Linnaeus's protests, Celsius's name stuck to the scale.

As is often the case, Aristotle was a founding figure in geodesy. He suggested that Earth was being held together because its material was falling toward its center, and forms a sphere as it does so. By the 17th century, this rudimentary description was fully explained by Isaac Newton's theory of gravitation: Earth's mass and everything on the surface was being pulled toward the center of gravity. There was still a question left unanswered. A centrifugal force is created as Earth spins, and this would make the planet bulge. But in which direction? Christiaan Huygens, a Dutch contemporary of Newton's, had suggested that Earth was flattened at the poles like an orange—the mathematical term used was "oblate spheroid"—and the gravitational calculations of Isaac Newton supported this view. Frenchman René Descartes thought the opposite, that Earth was prolate, more like a lemon, with pointed poles.

Mission to measure

A survey by Jacques Cassini, the director of the Paris Observatory, found that the distances covered by one degree of latitude (moving northward through France) appeared to increase. That suggested that Earth was more prolate. It was crucial to find the exact shape, not just for scientific purposes, but also to ensure that maps, and the lines of latitude and longitude marked on them, were accurate representations of the surface of the planet.

To find Earth's shape, scientists needed accurate measurements for Earth's polar and equatorial circumferences. If they were the same,

The northern part of the geodesic mission, which went to the European Arctic, was the first to discover the true shape of Earth in 1736.

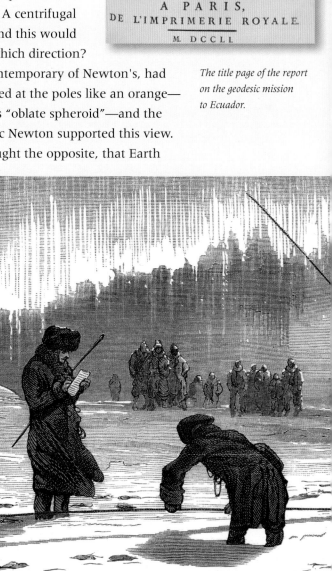

JOURNAL
DU
VOYAGE FAIT PAR ORDRE DU ROI,
A L'EQUATEUR,
SERVANT D'INTRODUCTION HISTORIQUE
A LA
MESURE
DES
TROIS PREMIERS DEGRÉS
DU MÉRIDIEN.
Par M. DE LA CONDAMINE.

Opposuit Natura Alpemque nivemque. Juven. Sat. X.

A PARIS,
DE L'IMPRIMERIE ROYALE.
M. DCC LI.

The title page of the report on the geodesic mission to Ecuador.

A DEGREE OF LATITUDE

Latitude is a measure of distance north or south of the Equator. On the curve of Earth's surface it is easiest to calculate and present this in degrees, the units used to measure angles (not temperature this time). Navigators had learned that they could find latitude from the angle of heavenly bodies. By the 18th century, they did this with a sextant (a device promoted in part by George Hadley's brother John). To simplify, let's imagine using the North Star to calculate latitude. This star is so called because it is (almost) directly above Earth's North Pole. When its altitude is 90°, i.e. straight up, your latitude is 90° N—you are at the North Pole. When the star's altitude is 0°, in other words it is on the horizon (just out of view), your latitude is also 0° and you are sailing on the Equator. It was not quite as straightforward for the Sun, which is the largest and brightest object in the sky—and the only one visible by day. However, pioneers of long-distance navigation compiled almanac tables that gave the latitude for every conceivable solar altitude for every day of the year. Accuracy was crucial; a few degrees out would result in being hundreds of kilometers out of position. In addition, mapmakers and scientists forming a mathematical model of the planetary surface needed to know the exact length on the surface corresponding to a disance of one degree. If Earth was oblate (blue) or prolate (yellow), the size of a degree of latitude would not be constant all over the planet.

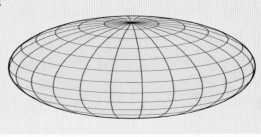

then the planet was a perfect sphere. However everyone suspected that one was bigger than the other. If the equatorial degree of latitude was larger, then Earth was oblate, but if the degree of latitude got bigger nearer the poles, the planet was prolate—and the difference between the equatorial and polar reading would give a rough estimate of how deformed Earth's sphere was.

To answer this fundamental question, French King Louis XV sent out two missions. The first was to measure a meridian arc at the Equator. In 1735, a team left for the Spanish territory of Quito (now Ecuador, a name that literally means "Equator" in Spanish) taking a total of four years to get back to France with their results. In the meantime, another team, including the Swede Anders Celsius (prior to making his name with his centigrade temperature scale, see box left), went to Lapland in Scandinavia, some of the closest land to the North Pole. There they measured a similar length of arc—the distance around a curved section of Earth—as the equatorial mission. Both results clearly showed that Huygens and Newton were correct. We live on an oblate planet that bulges in the middle and is flatter on the top and bottom.

An observation post replicating the one used by the French geodesic mission to Ecuador was built in 1836 to commemorate the 100-year-anniversary of the expedition.

31 Geological Maps

IN 1743, AN ENGLISH DOCTOR AND AMATEUR EARTH SCIENTIST CAME UP WITH A NEW WAY OF UNDERSTANDING THE LAND BENEATH OUR FEET. He drew a map that instead of showing rivers, roads, and towns, showed the layers of rocks.

A color version of William Smith's influential map was published in 1815.

The creator of this first geological map was called Christopher Packe, and his map of the Canterbury area (or as he put it *A Dissertation upon the Surface of the Earth, as delineated in a specimen of a Philosophico-Chorographical Chart of East-Kent*) passed by with little fanfare, but was presented to the Royal Society of London. Maps of mineral deposits and mining locations date back to antiquity, but Packe's map was different. His idea was to show where a certain rock strata reached the surface, and the boundaries where a new rock appeared at the surface. The previous rock disappeared from view in this location but it was still there, plunging unseen beneath the ground. Steno's principles of stratigraphy said that rock layers formed more or less horizontally, so what Packe's prototype map was able to show was that the layers had become angled and warped since their formation, and now met the surface a little like the grains on sawn wood.

More detail

Other geologists had similar ideas and made more elaborate and detailed geological maps. In 1746 Jean-Étienne Guettard created a mineralogical map of France, but this lacked the stratigraphy of Packe's chart. At the end of the 18th century, a mining engineer called William Smith produced a geological map of the whole of the Britain. It is said this map changed the world because its compelling graphics altered the way people viewed their planet.

In the 19th century, geological maps adopted the innovation of cross sections, like this one of Glencoul Thrust, in the Highlands of Scotland.

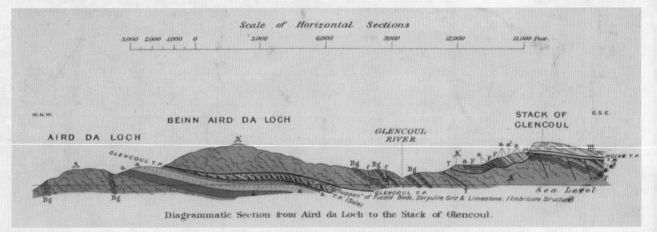

Scale of Horizontal Sections

Diagrammatic Section from Aird da Loch to the Stack of Glencoul.

32 Earthquakes

ANCIENT PEOPLE WERE ALL TOO FAMILIAR WITH EARTHQUAKES. THEY REMAIN THE MOST DESTRUCTIVE force on the planet, and we still struggle to predict them. A devastating earthquake in 1755 gave clues to what was going on.

Lisbon was hit with a triple disaster of earthquake, tsunami, and firestorm. John Michell correctly proposed that the 1755 quake had an epicenter on the seabed.

The earthquake in question devastated Lisbon, the capital of Portugal. Following the massive quake that created huge cracks in the city's roads and squares, the survivors took refuge down at the docks. About 40 minutes after the earthquake, a tsunami surged in from the sea, inundating the quays. Areas that were not flooded were then caught up in a firestorm started by all the candles that fell over when the ground shook. Lisbon and other coastal communities were devastated, up to 100,000 people were killed, and the kingdom of Portugal never really recovered its stature on the world stage.

Cause and observation

In 1760, the English polymath John Michell—he also dabbled in electromagnetism and astronomy and was an early proponent of what are now called black holes—presented a paper called *Conjectures concerning the Cause and Observations upon the Phaenomena of Earthquakes* to the Royal Society. It won him election as a fellow of that prestigious scientific club.

Based on research into the 1755 Lisbon quake, Michell's paper set out the basic understanding of earthquakes that is still valid today: an earthquake begins at a single point underground called the focus. At this location, rock strata have shifted all of a sudden, either at an existing crack in the strata or at a new one. (These discontinuities would later be called faults.) The point on the surface above the focus is called the epicenter, and Michell used his research into where and when the 1755 quake happened to surmise that earth tremors spread out from the epicenter as waves through Earth's rock, like the ripples on a pond.

Today, earthquakes are studied by seismologists who detect the direction and intensity of waves moving through the planet.

33 Why Ice Floats

ACCURATE THERMOMETERS SHOWED details of how materials change as the temperature goes up—or down. In the 1750s this revealed a very special property of water.

Only the tip of the iceberg is seen above the ocean. The ice is freshwater, with a considerably lower density than the saltwater ocean. Sea ice, which is frozen salty water, tends to form sheets on the surface of the ocean.

In the 1750s, a Scottish chemist called Joseph Black found that as ice is warmed its temperature rises, but when it starts to melt into water, the increase in temperature stops. Only when the ice is all gone will the added heat register as an increase in temperature (of the water this time). Black called this phenomenon latent heat. It shows that during melting, the heat energy is being used to break the chemical bonds that keep ice as a solid mass.

Ice takes up more room than the water that makes it. That is why frozen containers may crack. The increase in volume is due to the water molecules being rearranged as they link together into a solid. The same mass in a larger volume means that the density of ice is lower than that of water—and so ice floats in liquid water. No other naturally occurring solid material will float in its liquid form. In natural settings, that means that ice forms at the surface of bodies of water, which has far-reaching consequences. Surface ice insulates the water beneath and stops it freezing, providing living space for aquatic life even in winter. In addition, ice is exposed to sunlight, so melts. If it sank to the bottom of the ocean, then thick layers of ice would build up on the seabed, fundamentally changing Earth's geology and weather.

34 Igneous Rocks

WATCHING THE WAY MOLTEN GLASS COOLED CREATED THE KERNEL of an idea that became a central tenet in our understanding of the formation of rocks.

James Keir was a Scottish industrialist, who took a firm interest in the new sciences that were central to the Industrial Revolution that gripped Britain in his day. He was a leading figure in the Lunar Society, an informal gathering of like-minded intellectuals that included Erasmus Darwin (Charles's grandfather), James Watt (the steam engineer), and Benjamin Franklin during his days in

An engraving from 1778 shows lava forming columns of rock (basalt) as it meets the river water.

England. In 1776, Keir presented a paper proposing that today's rocks were formed in the past from molten lava, in the same kind of way that molten glass sets solid.

Today, rock formed this way is described as igneous, meaning "from fire." Igneous rocks formed from lava on the surface, such as basalt, cooled very fast on contact with water or air, and so have small crystals. Rocks that cool much more slowly in underground chambers filled with magma (which is only termed lava once it gets to the surface) include granite. They are characterized by having much larger crystals.

The edifices of Yosemite, such as El Capitan, are huge masses, or basoliths, of granite that formed underground only to be exposed at the surface when softer rocks around them eroded away.

35 Age of the Earth

A LITERAL READING OF THE BIBLE, with its long list of Abraham's family history, suggests that Earth was created in 4004 BCE. In 1779 CE, a French nobleman had an idea of how to verify this as the age of our planet.

The nobleman was Georges-Louis Leclerc, Comte de Buffon. He was the leading naturalist of his day, helping to overhaul the royal menagerie and botanical gardens near Paris. A generation or two ahead of Charles Darwin, the Comte also began piecing together ideas for a theory of evolution. This work led him to wonder about the origins of Earth and the Solar System. He rejected the age of Earth as set out by the Bible, and instead theorized that Earth was formed when a comet had hit the Sun, flinging out hot material. Since then the planet had steadily been losing heat. Volcanic activity was evidence that it was clearly still very hot beneath the surface, and he reasoned that Earth's magnetic field suggested the planet must contain a lot of iron. So he thought that he could use the rate at which this metal cooled to estimate the age of Earth. He heated a small sphere of iron to white heat, waited for it to cool, and then extrapolated his results—using a mathematical technique devised by Sir Isaac Newton—to find the time an Earth-sized sphere would take to cool. His answer of 75,000 years was still wrong, of course, but it was a first hint that the planet was much older than previously thought.

The Comte de Buffon's idea was inspired by the work that Isaac Newton had done 70 years before on the way iron and other red-hot substances cool down.

The Comte de Buffon was the director of the Jardin du Roi, the French royal botanical gardens.

36 A Theory of Earth

THE MODERN SCIENCE OF GEOLOGY BEGINS WITH THE WORK OF THE SCOTTISH FARMER AND ENGINEER JAMES HUTTON. In 1788 he published an overview of how rocks were formed in a book called *Theory of the Earth*.

During his work in the fields of the Scottish lowlands and while digging canals, Hutton got a good look at what lay beneath the ground. In the late 1750s, he began to consider how rocks formed. Hutton made the reasonable assumption that a rock with a particular composition deep underground had been created from a layer of fragments that had formed at the surface in the past. Those ancient materials were the same kinds of things that covered the surface now—stuff like sand, shells, and clay. This idea was a re-imagining of the work of Shen Kuo several centuries before (but it is unlikely Hutton knew of this Chinese thinker).

Uniformitarianism

Hutton's approach was that "the present is the key to the past." In 1785 he encapsulated his ideas in a theory that he called uniformitarianism. This says that the processes that formed rocks in the distant past are the same as the processes that can be seen going on in the present day. Hutton said that rock forms when layers

James Hutton spent nearly 30 years pondering how the features that he saw underground and at the surface related to the formation of rocks.

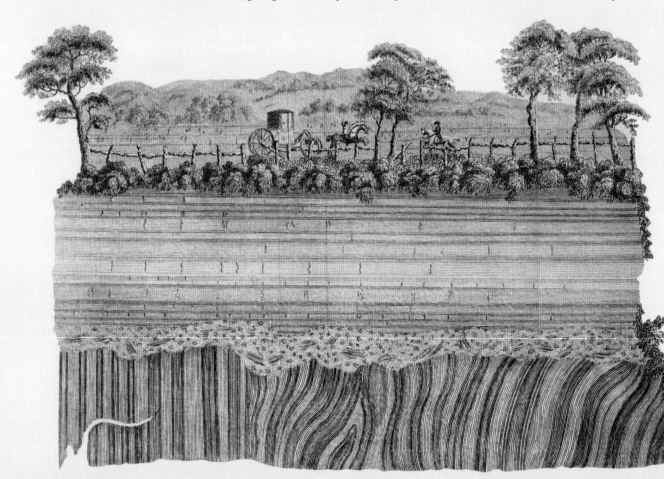

In 1787, James Hutton discovered a major break in the rock layers, or strata, which he called an unconformity. He went on to see the same break— now called Hutton's Unconformity—at various locations around Scotland. This drawing was made at Jedburgh. It reveals how older rock layers have been pushed to near vertical, and new horizontal ones formed on top.

of fragmented material, such as mud or sand, that cover the surface become buried by newer layers, or sediments, that form on top. Over a long period, the sediments are compressed until they bond together into a single piece of stone. Today, we call rocks formed like this "sedimentary." They include sandstones and limestones.

Crumbling to dust

Even rocks do not last forever. Sediments form in a number of ways, but the most common is that they flake away, or erode from older rocks. The weakening process, known as weathering, involves a combination of chemical, biological, and physical processes (such as wind and rain). Dust and grains are washed or blown away to form new sediments. The processes Hutton described were slow, and suggested that Earth was very old indeed.

Sedimentary rock · Sedimentation · Erosion · Igneous rock · Pressure · Cooling · Metamorphic rock · Melting · Magma

ROCK CYCLE

James Hutton's theory of uniformitarianism underwrites this modern picture of the way rocks are formed, transformed, and destroyed. As well as igneous and sedimentary rocks, the rock cycle includes metamorphic rocks which are transformed by heat and pressure (see more, page 119).

37 Neptunism

HOT ON THE HEELS OF JAMES HUTTON'S *THEORY OF THE EARTH*, CAME AN ALTERNATIVE THEORY. The German Abraham Gottlob Werner proposed that rocks all formed on the bottom of the sea.

Before Hutton's work had had a chance to spread through scientific thinking (it was not widely published until 1795), there were two rival schools of thought about the origins of rock. The Plutonists—they took their name from the Roman god of the underworld, who oversaw a hot volcanic kingdom— followed the idea that rocks were formed from hot volcanic activity, namely when lava and magma cooled. The Neptunists, led by Werner, were in thrall to the god of the ocean. They said that rocks formed gradually from the deposition of crystals on the seabed that were formed from chemicals dissolved in seawater. This process could be observed in the laboratory and in the creation of rocky formations in caves and cascades. Would it not also happen under the ocean as well? No one could say either way. The debate continued into the 19th century, until the Plutonist ideas won out as they were included as part of Hutton's broader theory.

Abraham Gottlob Werner suggested that Earth had begun as a ball of water, and had steadily grown into its current state from a core of rock at the center.

38 Extinction

WHILE IT BECAME AN ACCEPTED VIEW THAT FOSSILS WERE THE REMAINS OF ANIMALS THAT HAD DIED in the ancient past, it was assumed they belonged to species alive today. In 1796, Georges Cuvier proved otherwise.

Cuvier made drawings to compare the jaw anatomy of an Indian elephant (top right) with the extinct species, named as the mammoth, (bottom right).

Cuvier was an expert in vertebrate anatomy, and studied the fossil bones of what looked like rhinoceroses and elephants. (These fossils were dug up near Paris, which was evidence that French wildlife had been very different in the ancient past.) Cuvier was able to show that these skeletons belonged to different types of animals than lived today, anywhere on Earth. This was the first proof that life could become extinct. In Cuvier's view, animals had been created on Earth in several episodes, each ending with a catastrophe—he used the word "revolution"—which caused their extinctions. Others saw it as evidence that life was able to gradually change or evolve.

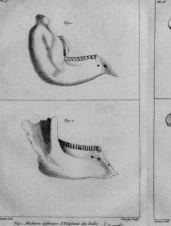

39 Classifying Clouds

A PHARMACIST BY PROFESSION, LUKE HOWARD WAS AN ENTHUSIASTIC AMATEUR IN OTHER FIELDS. He first took an interest in pollen, but then turned his attention skyward and had his head in the clouds.

WHAT IS A CLOUD?

A cloud is made of tiny droplets of water which are dispersed in the air. The droplets form around a solid core, a tiny speck of dust or ice that is floating in the air. Water vapor condenses around this core, and as the humidity increases—or temperature drops—the condensation goes up, and the droplets grow bigger. Eventually, the droplets are too heavy to float in the air, and they fall as rain. The cloud is a kind of mixture called a colloid, where the constituents are evenly spread but one of them (the water) is much larger than the other (the air molecules). This arrangement scatters light into a uniform white. Rainclouds appear dark and gray because the sunlight from above is reflected upward, away from the eye.

Howard was an Englishman and so had plenty of opportunity to see clouds of all kinds in the changeable British climate. In 1802 he presented the first version of his *Essay on the Modifications of Clouds*, and several later editions were to follow.

The essay set out the physical processes by which clouds formed: actions like evaporation, saturation, and condensation, with which Howard was well acquainted through his work in the chemistry lab. However, the lasting impact of Howard's work was the way he classified clouds, introducing names that we still use today (although extended; see more, page 72). Howard's system divides clouds into three main types:

the cirrus, the cumulus, and the stratus. Cirrus clouds are thin, wispy, and threadlike. The name comes from the Latin for "lock of hair." Howard said that cirrus are the first to appear in a blue sky. They are generally at high altitude and so do not really seem to move. Next come cumulus, which are named with the Latin word for "pile." Cumulus clouds are the fluffy ones that are generally low enough to appear to move appreciably across the sky in the wind. Finally come stratus, which Howard described as having a density somewhere between the other two. Stratus are the lowest of the three, and the term means "layer," which reflects the way they run horizontally, close to the horizon. Rather mysteriously, Howard called them "clouds of the night."

The essay then addressed when two cloud types appear to merge: Cirrocumulus and cirrostratus form when cirrus clouds descend. Cumulostratus, Howard said, look like a mushroom. A cloud formed by all three types—the cumulocirrostratus—was given a less complex name: nimbus. The nimbus is the kind of cloud people are most interested in because, according to Howard, this is the only type that produces precipitation.

Above are original drawings from an 1849 edition of Howard's cloud essay. From left to right: clouds gathering for a thunderstorm; cirrus above cumulostratus; the fog formed when a stratus reaches the ground.

This landscape painting by Edward Kenyon of a cloudy English day—showing cumulostratus—was made from sketches provided to the artist by Howard.

40 Wind Speeds and Storms

BY THE START OF THE 19TH CENTURY, TRANSOCEANIC TRAVEL WAS BECOMING ROUTINE. However, it was still a dangerous pursuit. In 1805, a sailor devised a system for judging the sea conditions so crews knew whether to press ahead or to seek shelter.

Above: Francis Beaufort so impressed with his scale and surveying skills that he was made the British Admiralty Hydrographer of the Navy after retiring from command.

Below: An original description of Beaufort's "Scale of Winds."

As well as moving up the ranks of the Royal Navy, the Irish seaman Francis Beaufort was specializing in a new field called hydrography. In 1795, the British government appointed the first official Hydrographer, Alexander Dalrymple, whose job was to measure and understand the oceans—the shape of the coasts, the depths of the seabed—and then put that all together to make it safer to navigate across the seas. In the early 1800s, Beaufort was in command of a warship sent to escort merchant ships making the long voyage back from India to Britain, and during this time he produced what he called a Scale of Winds—which is now also called the Beaufort Scale. It is still used today, especially in more extreme weather, as a shorthand for the power of a storm—a force 9 gale or force 12 hurricane—although, of course, modern navigators are furnished with more detailed meteorological information.

CUP ANEMOMETER

The Beaufort Scale is largely based on wind and sea conditions, but an accurate anemometer is also an essential tool. In 1846, the Irish inventor Thomas Romney Robinson designed a new anemometer, a four-cup version which incorporated a counter that tallied up the rotations. The curved cups also created aerodynamic forces that ensured the device spun smoothly, giving an accurate reading.

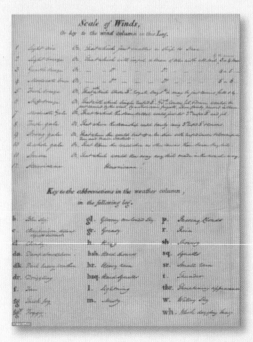

The Beaufort Scale

The scale divides winds into 13 "forces," defined by wind speed and how that can be assessed by the prevailing conditions. For example, Force 0 is no wind at all; Force 3 is a gentle breeze up to 19 km/h (12 mph), which creates a scattering of white horses on the surface of the ocean. Force 7 indicates winds of 50–61 km/h (32–38 mph). In these conditions the sea is rough with breaking waves, and the wind is strong enough to create streaks of spray. On land it would become hard to walk normally. Most people would find a Force 7 sea uncomfortable, but to a seasoned sailor, these are merely "moderate" conditions. Forces 8 and 9 are gales, with winds of up to 88 km/h (54 mph). Next comes the Force 10 storm. Rare inland, these winds of 102 km/h (63 mph) would uproot trees, and the rolling sea would become almost white with spray. Once the sea goes completely white you have reached the end of the scale, a Force 12 hurricane, with winds above 118 km/h (73 mph).

41 Fossil Records

AFTER PROVING THAT THE ANIMALS (AND PLANTS) IN ANCIENT TIMES WERE DIFFERENT TO THOSE ALIVE NOW, Georges Cuvier teamed up with a mining engineer to show that fossils can tell us the history of Earth.

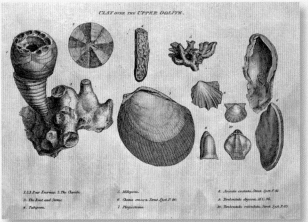

William Smith, who was one of the first people to create a geological map when he drew one in 1815, produced these detailed records of the fossils he found in different strata.

Following his discovery at the end of the 18th century that species can become extinct, Cuvier then worked for many years with Alexandre Brongniart to map the fossils in the rocks around Paris. Brongniart was a mineralogist who worked at the city's mining school, so his job was to survey the rocks that lay beneath the region. This stratigraphy—based on the earlier work of Steno—was then embellished with the different kinds of fossils in each layer.

Biostratigraphy

The pair's early results were ready for the public in 1808 but the final report took until 1811. The fossil record that Brongniart and Cuvier found showed that in the distant past, the Paris Basin had periodically changed between being a seafloor, dry land, and freshwater habitats. To Cuvier this was evidence of his catastrophic theory of life on Earth, but it was also a proof of the concept of biostratigraphy. This seeks to determine the age of rock layers—at least in relation to each other—by applying the principle of faunal succession to the fossils they contain (see box, right).

Later work in this area has revealed index fossils, which are lifeforms that are common in rocks of a certain age. If you find an index fossil in an American rock, it tells you that this rock is of similar age to a Chinese rock that contains the same index fossil. As a result, the fossil record can be used to connect geological formations around the world and begin to tell us about distant events in the long history of our planet.

FAUNAL SUCCESSION

The fossil record is based on the principle of faunal succession, which says that the fossil remains—of flora as well as fauna—appear in distinct layers, with older species always featuring in a deeper stratum than newer species. It is impossible, therefore, for a human skeleton to appear in the same rock as a dinosaur fossil. However, geological forces may sometimes fold and buckle younger rock layers until they are underneath older ones.

42 Climatology

ALEXANDER VON HUMBOLDT WAS A GENTLEMAN EXPLORER, who opened up much of the world to scientific scrutiny. One of his lasting legacies was to observe climate at the global level.

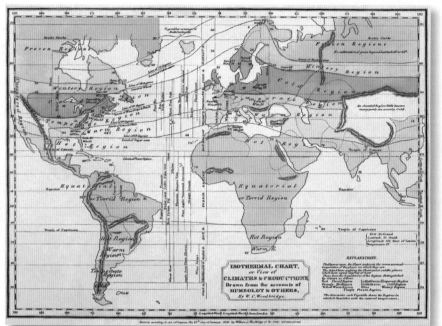

ISOTHERMAL CHART,
or View of
CLIMATES & PRODUCTIONS,
Drawn from the accounts of
HUMBOLDT & OTHERS,
By W. C. Woodbridge.

William Channing Woodbridge created this color map of climate regions from the isotherm data supplied by Humboldt.

Friedrich Wilhelm Heinrich Alexander von Humboldt was from Prussia, a German-speaking state that once ran from the North Sea, along the Baltic coast to the frontier with Russia. Some major world events mean that this state no longer exists on the map. However, Humboldt's name is a common feature on maps today. There are 17 geographical features—bays, waterfalls, caves, etc—named for him, plus a similar number of towns, at least four universities, dozens of high schools, and even an ocean current that runs north along the Pacific coast of South America.

What did this 19th-century polymath do to deserve all these accolades? For one thing, his main expeditions, between 1799 and 1804, were made mostly to the Americas, where, at the time, many things did not have European names. However, Humboldt also personally started several areas of earth science such as the fields of biogeography, climatology, and monitoring changes in Earth's magnetism.

Mapping climate

Biogeography explores how the distribution of animals and plants relates to the climate. To do this Humboldt took a rounded view of the sciences, seeking to bring together biology, climate studies, and geology to find answers. It took him many years to analyse the information he had gathered on his expeditions to the Americas and combine it with data from other sources to create a global geographic picture.

In 1817 he pioneered the use of isotherms on maps. These are lines that connect points on Earth that have the same average temperature. An isothermal map reveals that average temperature exists in relatively tidy bands that circle the globe,

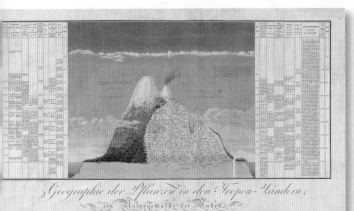

creating climate regions, although early versions were somewhat simplistic. Humboldt described the warmest regions around the Equator as torrid, and heading progressively north and south, the regions became hot, warm, temperate, cold, wintry, and frozen. The trend is obvious enough, and this map, the first of its kind since the discovery and mapping of all major landmasses, was a starting point for climatology, a science that seeks to understand how weather patterns vary across the planet.

Biogeography

A major interest of Humboldt's was to understand how different wildlife communities of plants and animals were associated with each climate zone. Today, this pursuit has been refined into the idea of biomes, which are climate zones that are defined by the kinds of habitats they support—and include factors other than average temperature, such as rainfall and seasonal changes. Familiar biomes include tropical rainforest and deserts—both of which would largely fall into Humboldt's torrid zone—and tundra and grassland, which are in colder and drier locations.

Looking into the past

A map of present-day climate, and the biogeographic regions that go along with them, becomes a valuable reference when we begin to look at the fossil record beneath. The kinds of fossil found show how habitats have changed in the geologic past—as Cuvier had found in Paris—and that also reveals how climate regions have shifted around. This kind of thinking would prove to be inspirational to Charles Darwin, who made an expedition similar to Humboldt's a generation later and began to wonder where all the different life forms came from. Other scientists were more interested in what causes the apparent changes in climate zones. Was it because the whole planet got warmer, colder, wetter, or drier? Or was it because land that is currently in the torrid equatorial region was once somewhere else on the planet's surface in the very distant past? All these questions needed answers.

Alexander von Humboldt created a map of the plant life on the slopes of Chimborazo, a tall volcano in Ecuador, noting how it changed as altitude brought more extreme weather conditions.

A painting from 1810 shows Alexander von Humboldt (standing) at the foot of Chimborazo, a volcano in Ecuador. Due to the equatorial bulge of Earth, the summit of this mountain is the farthest point on Earth's surface from the center of the planet.

Basalt prisms at Santa María Regla in Mexico, as recorded in Alexander von Humboldt's travel diary to that country in 1803.

43 Weather Maps

THE WEATHER MAPS BROADCAST AFTER THE TV NEWS OR SHOWN IN NEWSPAPERS ARE INSTANTLY RECOGNIZABLE—AND GENERALLY FORGETTABLE. They are based on synoptic maps first devised in the 1820s by Heinrich Brandes.

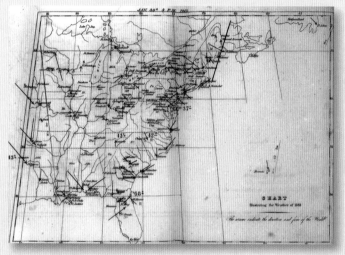

This weather map from 1843 is the oldest one showing the USA. It shows the weather on January 30, 1843, and was produced by James Pollard Espy for the Surgeon General of the United States Army.

As well as giving us the weather map, Brandes, a German scientist, also made another contribution to meteorology—the study of weather phenomena. This second contribution was that meteorology has nothing to do with meteors. After graduating in 1800, Brandes worked as an astronomer—among other fields of interest—and he was able to show that meteors, or shooting stars, were so high in the atmosphere that they had no impact on the weather effects that were experienced at the surface.

Nevertheless, the term meteorology stuck, (although Brande would have used the German term Witterungskunde, so perhaps he did not care too much about that). Brande went on to make his second contribution to the science 20 years later. Today, he is regarded as the father of "synoptic meteorology," which is admittedly an accolade that does not resonate far beyond professional weather forecasters.

The synopsis of weather conditions on the East Coast of the USA at 10 p.m. on March 12, 1888, shows the passage of a storm that resulted in the Great Blizzard of 1888, also known as the Great White Hurricane.

A big picture

The word synoptic means "seen together," and a synoptic map—as pioneered by Brandes in a book called *Beiträge zur Witterungskunde* (Contributions to Meteorology)—is a large-scale summary (or synopsis) of the weather conditions at one specific moment in the near past. Brandes's chart lacked much detail, mostly because the ability to observe and collate weather information from a wide area was limited in his day. A modern synoptic map covers a region of the surface that is around 1,000 km (620 miles) wide, and it contains information about temperature, wind speed and direction, and air pressure at various locales within the region. There might also be other information such as cloud cover. This large-scale snapshot of atmospheric conditions can then be used to forecast general changes to the weather.

44 Dinosaur

IN 1822, A FOSSIL HUNT IN A QUARRY IN ENGLAND PRODUCED A DISCOVERY that would change our view of natural history. The distant past was not like now, but a strange world ruled by what look like giant lizards!

Early interpretations of the iguanodon skeleton saw it posed on its back legs while it gathered food with its forelegs. However, it actually spent most of its time on all fours.

Today we know that these ancient creatures belonged to a separate group of reptiles to lizards. In 1842, these monsters were given a suitable name—the dinosaurs—which is derived from the Greek words for "terrible lizard." People had been coming across bones and teeth of dinosaurs throughout history, but without knowing what they were. In ancient China they were called "dragon bones."

Fossil records are dominated by shellfish, which have mineral-rich shells that lend themselves to preservation in sediments. (In fact, entire strata of limestones and chalks can be formed from layers of seashells.) However, as fossil hunters took a more methodical approach, it became clear that as well as shellfish, there were skeletal remains of huge, extinct animals, including giant reptiles, which had once populated the Earth. Among the first to be unearthed were ichthyosaurs, which were found in 1811, (and are now understood as separate from dinosaurs and other giant reptiles).

The first dinosaur to be identified was discovered by English paleontologist Gideon Mantell at a fossil-rich quarry in Sussex, first as a single tooth and then as a complete skeleton. This was a giant land animal with teeth like a present-day iguana, so Mantell called it iguanadon ("iguana-tooth"). Since Mantell's time, dinosaurs have never lost their fascination. Despite their name, they are not actually lizards, but are more closely related to crocodiles.

Over 1,000 fossil species are now known, and probably more are waiting to be discovered. Dinosaurs are said to have become extinct about 66 million years ago. But, in fact, there are still around 10,000 dinosaur species flourishing today. We just call them birds.

MARY ANNING

Mary Anning collected and sold fossils in Lyme Regis, on the south coast of England, where the cliffs are rich in fossils. She became an expert at finding extinct marine reptiles such as the fish-like ichthyosaur. As a woman, and without a university education, she was prevented from participating in the scientific life of her time, but members of the scientific community now appreciate how crucial her discoveries and insights were.

Mary Anning worked with William Buckland to study the fossil poop of dinosaurs and other extinct creatures. Stone made from droppings is called coprolite.

45 Principles of Geology

PRINCIPLES
OF
GEOLOGY,
BEING
AN ATTEMPT TO EXPLAIN THE FORMER CHANGES
OF THE EARTH'S SURFACE,
BY REFERENCE TO CAUSES NOW IN OPERATION.
BY
CHARLES LYELL, Esq., F.R.S.
VOLUME THE SECOND.
LONDON:
JOHN MURRAY, ALBEMARLE-STREET.

Left: The title page of Lyell's book which, in full, is titled: Principles of Geology: being an attempt to explain the former changes of the Earth's surface, by reference to causes now in operation.

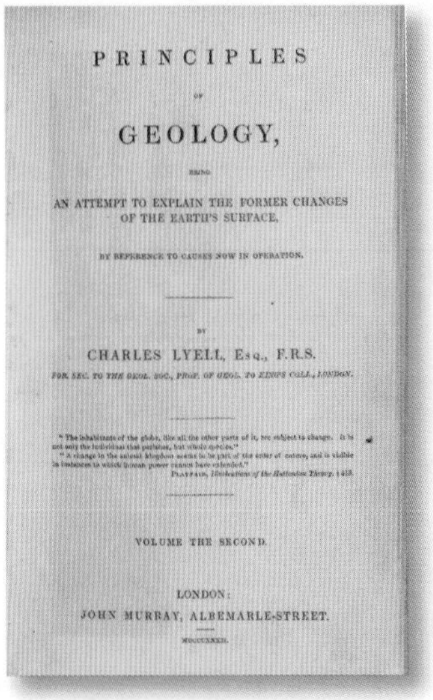

The groundbreaking theories of James Hutton concerning ground-making (or how rocks formed) from sediments, had received little attention. A bestselling book in the 1830s changed all that.

The book was called *Principles of Geology,* and its author, Charles Lyell, extended the ideas from Hutton's *Theory of the Earth* 45 years before. This required three volumes with the final one being released in 1833. Lyell's approach was to use the principles of uniformitarianism, which says we can understand how ancient rock formations were created by looking at processes happening in the present, on a much wider, global scale. While he made no claim to the central theory, and was criticized for creating a too theoretical work rather than one based on evidence, Lyell's books had a big impact on the popular imagination. Two avid readers were Robert FitzRoy, a naval captain and early weather forecaster, and his friend Charles Darwin.

46 Ice Ages

Visitors to the valleys of the Alps or other tall mountain ranges might wonder how such massive boulders have ended up in the middle of a field or village. How did they get there? The answer revealed another secret of Earth's hidden past.

Mountain people explain that they were moved there by the local glacier, a frozen torrent of ice that flows slowly down from the peaks. The leading edge of the glacier eventually melts, depositing an assortment of rubble that has been carried with the ice. This forms a deposit of rocks called a moraine, and in the 18th century several European researchers, in the Alps and further afield, recognized rock formations far from any glacier as being moraines. Surely at some point in the distant past, ice had brought those rocks there. This was the explanation offered by James Hutton, among others.

Worldwide deep freeze

In 1824, the Danish-Norwegian geologist Jens Esmark suggested that the global climate changed, creating periods

ICE CORES

A glacier, also known as a polar ice sheet, grows slowly as thin layers of ice form on its surface year after year. These layers work a bit like the growth rings of a tree. By drilling deep into a glacier, the ice layers revealed can help tell how old a glacier is. This is what Louis Agassiz did in the 1840s—using the augur pictured here. Since then, ice core drilling has become much more advanced. As well as dating ice, the cores are a time capsule of the chemicals present in the air and water when the ice layer formed. These include traces of dust from volcanoes and other catastrophes, and bubbles of ancient air, which reveal carbon dioxide levels in the past.

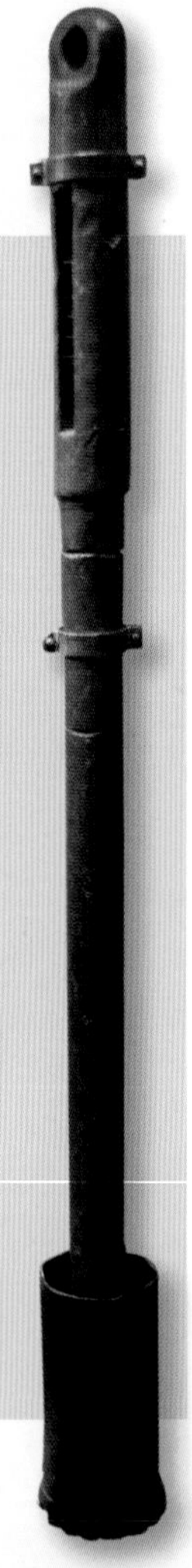

of cold that spread glaciers far and wide. The geologists of the time ruminated on this idea, occasionally offering more evidence for ancient glaciations. In the 1830s, a German botanist called Karl Friedrich Schimper spent many days exploring the mountains for his study of moss, but he turned his attention to the boulders they grew on. Schimper believed that these rocks were evidence of an ice age. He told his Swiss friend Louis Agassiz all about his ideas, and pair began to work together. In 1837, Schimper coined the term "ice age" for when the world was highly glaciated. Later that year Agassiz presented their theory to the Swiss naturalist society. It was met with opposition, because it contradicted the view then that the world was gradually cooling down from its red-hot creation. Agassiz set off to prove his detractors wrong, and in 1840 published *Studies on Glaciers*—which did not mention Schimper (or any other influences). That put ice-age researchers at loggerheads, and the theory was only fully accepted with the work of James Croll and his 1875 book *Climate and Time, in Their Geological Relations.*

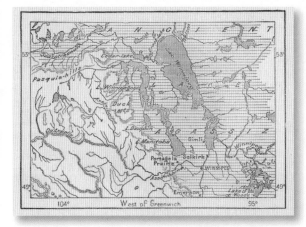

This map from 1885 shows the location of Lake Agassiz, a vast ancient glacial lake that covered a part of Canada, named for the leading ice-age researcher.

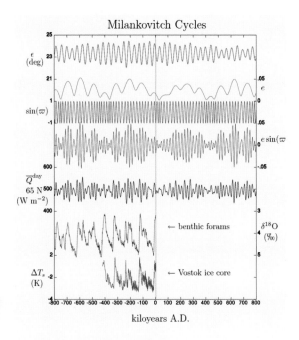

MILANKOVITCH CYCLES

Named with an anglicized version of Milutin Milanković, the Serbian geophysicist who suggested them in the 1920s, these cycles arise from the cumulative effects of the way Earth wobbles as it spins and shifts gradually in its orbit. Over thousands of years, these create a cyclical variation in the amount of sunlight hitting the Earth. Ice ages and other climatic extremes are the result.

The discovery of ice ages began when scientists took summer vacations in the high mountains of Europe, and visited glacial valleys.

47 Weather Fronts

A CHANGE IN THE WEATHER HAPPENS WHEN MASSES OF AIR OF DIFFERENT TEMPERATURES MEET. The leading edge of the air masses are called their "fronts"—a relatively modern idea that has a surprisingly old origin.

Weather broadcasters often explain their forecasts in terms of weather fronts. This idea was firmly developed in the 1920s, mostly by a Norwegian school of meteorologists who knew a thing or two about bad weather. However, the central idea, that unsettled weather, such as rain or hail, is caused by a wall of warm, wet air meeting a zone of cold, dry air coming the other way, had already been proposed by Elias Loomis in 1841. Loomis was a mathematician who dabbled in many fields, so it is perhaps unsurprising that meteorologists did not pay much attention to this particular idea at the time.

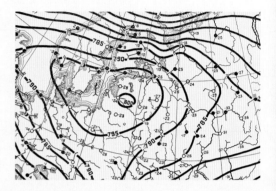

A weather map from the Soviet era shows a high-pressure zone over western Russia and northern Europe. High-pressure areas are associated with warm fronts.

Moving air

Weather fronts are most active to the north and south of the tropical and equatorial zones. Cold fronts move from west to east, while warm fronts move toward the North or South poles. Cold fronts are pushed along by air that is denser than that which pushes warm fronts and so move faster, bringing short rain showers with them. On the other hand, warm fronts are more likely to result in fog.

In his 1880 book, A Treatise on Meteorology, *Elias Loomis, set out the five-part life cycle of a waterspout—an ocean-going tornado—as he saw it: formation of a dark spot on the water surface; spiral pattern on the water surface; formation of a spray ring; development of the visible condensation funnel, and ultimately decay.*

48 Geological Time Scale

THE CONCEPT OF USING ROCK STRATA AND THE FOSSILS THEY CONTAIN AS A RECORD OF PAST GEOLOGICAL EVENTS was becoming well established in the mid-18th century. In 1841, John Phillips put it all together to make a complete history of the planet.

The work of Steno, Cuvier, and Mantell (to name but a few) had produced a wealth of information about the relative ages of different rock strata. Phillips was perhaps most influenced by the work of William Smith, the mining engineer turned geologist, who was his maternal uncle, and to whom he was apprenticed as a geological mapmaker. Phillips carved out a career in his own right as a paleontologist and curator, and in 1840 he was assigned to a geological survey being made of Great Britain. He became interested in fossils described as paleozoic—meaning "old life." The following year, Phillips published the first geological time scale. He divided the past into the Paleozoic Period for older life; more recent fossils, such as those of dinosaurs, were defined at the time to belong to the Age of Reptiles, which was followed by the Age of Mammals, which brought us up to the present day. Phillips re-termed the former as the Mesozoic Period, meaning "middle life," and the latter the Cenozoic, meaning "new life".

Before Phillips introduced the basis of today's time scale, the past was divided in a number of ways. One scheme included the Age of Reptiles, proposed by Gideon Mantell, who discovered the first dinosaur.

John Phillips was raised by his uncle, who was the renowned British geologist William Smith.

The modern time scale

Phillips's plan remains the basis of today's time scale (shown in detail on page 120). His three periods are now eras, divided into a total of 12 periods, all defined by the fossil record. Seven earlier eras also include the period of Earth's history before complex life evolved.

49 Manual of Mineralogy

IN 1848, THE AMERICAN GEOLOGIST JAMES DWIGHT DANA PUBLISHED THE ***MANUAL OF MINERALOGY,*** the first comprehensive guide to the minerals that occur in nature.

An original diagram from Dana's Manual of Mineralogy *showing the many different shapes of mineral crystals.*

Rocks are mere assemblages of minerals. Understand the chemical and physical nature of those natural compounds, and you discover how the rocks formed. The difficulty is that identifying one mineral from another can be as much an art as it is a science, especially when they are minute specks in rocks. Dana's 1848 work was the first foray into this complex world. It defined each mineral according to several features, from color and hardness to crystal structure and chemical composition. Today Dana's methods have been superseded by the Nickel-Strunz system.

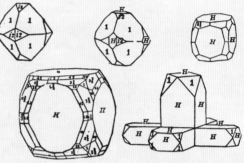

50 Continental Shelf and Beyond

IN 1807 PRESIDENT THOMAS JEFFERSON SET UP THE COAST SURVEY TO MAP **THE SHORES AND SEABED** around the USA. In the 1840s, while researching the route of the Gulf Stream, the Survey made a deep discovery.

The U.S. Coast Survey mapped the seabed by using a technique called depth sounding. Traditionally, that was done simply by dropping over the side of a boat a long, thin rope with a lead weight, or plummet, on the end. Down the weight went until it touched bottom. If 183 cm—2 yards or 6 six feet—of rope was played out, then that water was one fathom deep. Generally speaking, coastal waters were more than this, gradually getting deeper further from shore and reaching a depth of around 150 fathoms.

A decent nautical chart was needed for safe navigation near shore to show deep channels and prevent groundings. However, soundings far out to sea seldom hit bottom—the open ocean is very deep. Even today, using radar and sonar-based sounding equipment, we are mostly in the dark about anything smaller than 5 km (3.11 miles) across in the deep ocean. However, in 1849, the U.S. Coast Survey—using mechanical sounding machines for greater accuracy (see box, right)—found

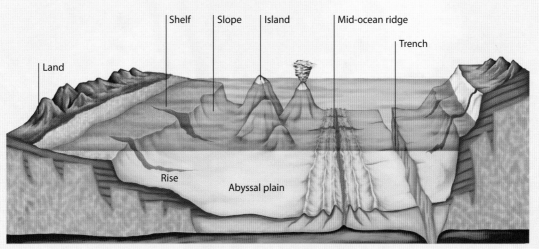

Land · Shelf · Slope · Island · Mid-ocean ridge · Trench · Rise · Abyssal plain

The seabed is not bland and uniform. It has mountains, volcanoes, and canyons just like dry land.

that the seabed along the East Coast was like a shelf. It stayed relatively flat, and then plunged downward out of reach of the sounding equipment. The shallow region is the continental shelf, and the American surveyors had found that it gives way to the continental slope. This was just the beginning of the discovery of an entirely new landscape submerged by the sea.

Continental margin

TRINCOMALEE
CEYLON

NAUTICAL MILES
DEPTHS IN FATHOMS

SUBMARINE CANYON

In 1857, soundings off the coast of California revealed the first example of a submarine canyon—what is now called Monterey Canyon. Underwater canyons, such the Trincomalee Canyon in Sri Lanka, shown above, are common features cutting through the continental slope and opening out onto the rise. Their submerged features are as large as anything on land.

The seabed submerged by coastal waters is still part of the thick continental landmass. The crust that forms the deep ocean floor is considerably thinner— hence the immense ocean basin that is filled with water. The continental slope is the boundary between the two types of crust, connecting the shallow coastal seas with the deep ocean. Continental shelves can extend 320 km (200 miles) from the shore before reaching the edge, or "shelf break." If the ocean were drained of water, this edge of the shelf would be the starkest boundary on Earth's surface.

The continental slope goes down at least 2,000 m (6,500 ft), to where the continental rise begins. This is a more gentle slope that leads to the abyssal plain, the flat seabed that is about 6,000 m (20,000 feet) down. (Only ocean trenches go deeper than this.) The rise is formed mostly from sediment that has washed off the shelf far above for millions of years—or been broken off by calamitous earthquakes resulting in an undersea rock fall.

SOUNDING MACHINE

Several designs of mechanical sounding machine were invented to service the growing fleets of the world. The most successful was invented in 1802 by Edward Massey, a clockmaker from England. The machine was fitted to the same rope as the plummet, which pulled it into the deep. As it sank, water flooded through a small rotor, which worked a dial that counted the increase in depth. This counter stopped once on the sea floor and was hauled up to be read.

51 Ocean Currents

WHILE THINKING OF WAYS TO STANDARDIZE THE COLLECTION OF WIND AND WEATHER DATA AT SEA, an American navigation expert hit upon a plan to map the ocean currents more accurately. All he needed was the cooperation of every ship at sea.

Johann Zahn's world map of 1696 contains an early attempt to depict ocean currents.

Accurate information on the wind and other average weather conditions that could be expected from region to region was a valuable resource for ocean-going vessels. The superintendent of the Depot of Charts and Instruments of the U.S. Navy, Matthew Fontaine Maury, who had been part of the first official U.S. circumnavigation of Earth, was acutely aware that whatever information was available was highly unreliable. In 1853, Maury launched the International Maritime Conference, holding the first meeting in Brussels, Belgium. There, international standards for taking weather measurements aboard ships were established, and, crucially, conference members also agreed a system for sharing it all.

Ahead of the game

Maury's initiative was the first step in creating a global dataset of weather information. When we talk about changes in global climate today, the starting point was the reliable database of air and sea temperatures that Maury began in the 1850s, and which has been continued and extended ever since. However, Maury had already got a head start.

Matthew Fontaine Maury's knowledge of ocean currents was put to the test when a U.S. navy troop ship went missing in a storm in the 1860s. Maury calculated how the survivors would be drifting and directed rescuers to that location. His predictions were perfect!

A map of the major ocean currents. Red arrows show warm currents that generally flow from the tropical regions, while the blue arrows are cold waters from polar areas.

His promising career at sea had been cut short in 1839 by a debilitating leg injury, and so he began gathering as much information as possible about ocean conditions, with the aim of creating more accurate navigation charts for those who could go to sea. An important detail was the nature of ocean currents, or as Maury (a committed Christian) saw them, the "Paths of the Seas" as they are described in the Psalms.

He studied old ships' logs, gleaning useful information from more than a million pieces of data to build a detailed picture of the speed and direction of ocean currents at different times of year—and the impact of winds on navigation along the currents. (He even tracked the movements of whales in the hope they would lead to an ice-free seaway through the Arctic: they did not.) Maury presented his findings in 1851 as *Sailing Directions and Physical Geography of the Seas and Its Meteorology*, which was given free to any American ship that agreed to keep a daily weather record and also to deploy weighted flasks known as 'drift bottles' into the sea at designated places. These were designed to float just under the surface so they would not be affected by the wind. Any bottles found by another ship or along the coast were sent back to Maury, who used their start and end points to refine his chart of ocean currents.

Maury's original Brussels conference in 1853 grew into today's World Meteorological Organization, part of the United Nations and headquartered in Geneva.

52 Human Relatives

AMONG THE FOSSILS OF OUTLANDISH EXTINCT BEASTS, PALEONTOLOGISTS OCCASIONALLY UNEARTHED THE REMAINS OF ANCIENT HUMANS. In 1856, anatomical analysis revealed that these bones were not quite that simple.

In 1829 the fossil of a partial human skull was found in Engis cave in Belgium. Then in 1848 a full skull was dug up in a quarry in Gibraltar. It was assumed they were the remains of a human being like you and me, a *Homo sapiens*, only one that lived many thousands of years ago. However the next discovery would show something else. In 1856, a partial human skeleton was found in a cave in the Neander Valley, or Neanderthal, in western Germany's Rhineland. The Neanderthal 1 specimen consisted of a skull cap, two thigh bones, three bones from the right arm, two of the left, and fragments of the pelvis, shoulder, and ribs. The naturalist Johann Carl Fuhlrott and the anatomist Hermann Schaaffhausen showed that they belonged to a species that was related to ours, but not the same. Following further work in 1864, our extinct cousins eventually became known as Neanderthals, or *Homo neanderthalenis*. The earlier Engis and Gibraltar finds were also revealed as Neanderthals, who lived in Europe until about 37,000 years ago—for part of the time sharing the territory with modern humans. Today, more than a dozen extinct *Homo* species have been identified, once living all over Africa, Europe, Asia, and the Indo-Pacific islands.

Ancient human fossils are often found in caves, where they have been undisturbed for thousands of years. This has led to the concept of "cave men," but our ancestors did not habitually live in caves, that is just where we are more likely to find remains.

53 Weather Forecast

TO MANY OF US, BEING ABLE TO PREDICT TOMORROW'S WEATHER helps us know whether to plan a day at the beach or to pack a raincoat. But, in the early days, weather forecasts could be a matter of life or death.

The person who coined the term weather "forecast" was the British naval captain Robert FitzRoy. FitzRoy had been the protégé of Francis Beaufort, whose Wind Force Scale from the 1800s was a helpful system for judging conditions at sea in the here-and-now, but could not say what would happen next. In 1854, FitzRoy, having retired from command, set up the Meteorological Office for the British government. Its job was to gather standardized weather data from British shipping with the aim of including climate information on sea charts.

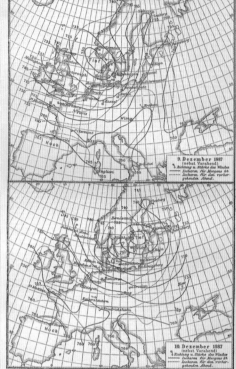

Opportunity arises

Later that year, a great storm hit the Black Sea. Supply ships carrying winter provisions for the French and British forces fighting the Russians in the Crimean War were lost. The French astronomer Urbain Le Verrier was able to show that the storm's eastward path across Europe was clear in the weather data collated after the incident. If this data could have been put together into a synoptic map within hours, instead of weeks, the Crimean fleet could have been saved. So the newly invented telegraph network was put to work to carry observation data to new weather observatories. FitzRoy's "Met Office" became the world's first—and longest lasting—weather forecaster. By 1861 it was issuing weather warnings by telegraph, and publishing a daily forecast in *The Times* of London (as it still does today).

A weather map for northern Europe from the 1880s. The curved lines are isobars, connecting places with equal air pressure. The maps show how conditions change from one day to the next and can be used to predict what will happen in future.

VOYAGE OF THE BEAGLE

Before becoming the pioneer of weather forecasting, Robert FitzRoy had the command of HMS *Beagle*, a small sloop that was used as a naval survey ship. Its second voyage, from 1831 to 1836, saw FitzRoy circumnavigate the world via Cape Horn, New Zealand, and Australia. He took with him a civilian companion, called Charles Darwin, who used the voyage to compare and contrast animals from across the globe, a pursuit that inspired his famous theory of evolution.

54 Exploring Altitude

WEATHER IS AN ATMOSPHERIC PHENOMENON, AND SO TO UNDERSTAND IT, IT MAKES SENSE to go up and have a closer look at all that air. Two early aerial explorers who did so only just made it home alive.

Coxwell and Glaisher's balloon voyage to the "aerial ocean" came close to ending in disaster as they flew so high that the thin air could not support life.

FIRST FLIGHT

The first balloons capable of carrying passengers were built by the French Montgolfier brothers. The first aeronauts flew in 1783 aboard their paper and silk craft, but they were not human. Instead, the balloon crew was a sheep, a duck, and a rooster, and each was selected for their physical attributes. The duck would be unaffected by altitude, while the rooster was a bird but one that could not fly high. The sheep was the stand-in for a human. All three were unaffected by the eight-minute flight.

In 1862, the British Association for the Advancement of Science suggested an expedition be made to explore the "aerial ocean." Henry Coxwell, the country's leading "aeronaut," was appointed to fly an enormous hydrogen balloon (2,600 m³; 93,000 cubic feet) designed to go higher than anyone had yet flown. The other member of the crew was the scientist James Glaisher, who would use a barometer to calculate altitude as indicated by the drop in pressure, and also plot the corresponding fall in temperature.

The crew also carried six homing pigeons, and planned to release them one by one as they ascended. The vast balloon rose quickly and the team was above the clouds in just 12 minutes. All was well as they admired the incredible view of the cloud cover below—something familiar to people today who fly by air, but back then something few had seen. At 4.83 km (3 miles or 15,840 feet) up, Glaisher began to release his pigeons. At 6.44 km or 4 miles, the pigeon struggled to fly, and at 8 km (5 miles), the birds simply fell from the balloon. At this point, Glaisher reported feeling "balloon sick" and was about to warn Coxwell when he became unconscious. Coxwell, a younger man, was less affected but had lost all feeling in his hands. He managed to open safety valves with his teeth to release hydrogen, and within about 20 minutes, the aircraft was back on the ground, with both the crew revived. Later analysis suggested that the pair had reached an altitude of 11.3 km (37,000 feet), which is near the cruising height of a jet airliner today, and far higher than Mount Everest. The air pressure up there is a fifth of the pressure at sea level, with too little oxygen to sustain the body, and the thin air holds little heat so the temperature is at most –40°C (-40°F).

55 Hurricane

WHAT BECAME THE NATIONAL WEATHER SERVICE IN THE UNITED STATES WAS SET UP IN 1870, AND THINGS GOT BUSY STRAIGHTAWAY. In 1873 the service issued the first of many hurricane warnings, and it has been leading the research into these giant storms ever since.

FUJIWHARA EFFECT

Named after Sakuhei Fujiwhara, the Japanese meteorologist who described it in 1921, the Fujiwhara Effect occurs when two storm systems get close enough that their winds pull them together so they orbit each other. The storms then change direction and eventually merge, potentially into a much larger and more dangerous storm. The effect is rare and happens only every few years.

The Weather Bureau of the United States was set up by President Ulysses S. Grant with a mission to "provide for taking meteorological observations at the military stations in the interior of the continent and at other points in the States and Territories … and for giving notice on the northern Lakes and on the seacoast by magnetic telegraph and marine signals, of the approach and force of storms." The new agency was under the auspices of the Secretary of War because it required military discipline to get the right results. (The Bureau has been through many changes since then, and is now the National Weather Service, part of NOAA, the National Oceanic and Atmospheric Administration; see more, page 101.)

The chief meteorologist was Cleveland Abbe, who had already started weather forecasting by using weather data sent by Western Union and the Cincinnati Chamber of Commerce. Abbe had consistently lobbied his bosses to provide him with the means to research weather phenomena so he could figure out how to predict them.

Storm season

In June 1873, the Bureau got wind of a storm moving through the Caribbean. It was nothing too bad, but in August, a major hurricane moved up the East Coast, finally decaying off Newfoundland, and September saw two more hurricanes striking Florida.

At the time, the world's leading authority on hurricanes was Benito Viñes, a Cuban priest, who ran a meteorological observatory in Havana. In 1877 he published a method of using wave and cloud motions to forecast hurricanes. It did little to help: 1893 was the deadliest in U.S. history as a series of major storms hit the East Coast. The U.S. Weather Bureau responded in 1898 with a hurricane warning center at Kingston, Jamaica, soon relocated to Havana, which is more prone to hurricanes. Two years later a hurricane hit Galveston, Texas, killing at least 8,000 people.

In the 1870s, ocean-going vessels were ill equipped to withstand hurricane conditions.

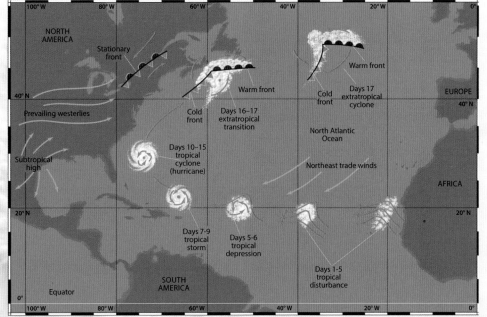

The strongest winds of all are in the eye wall, an immense circular cloud that surrounds a clear zone, with light winds and clear skies at the heart of the storm.

Atlantic hurricanes form far out in the ocean from weather systems emerging from the Sahara Desert. As they start out as low-pressure "tropical depressions," weather watchers monitor their westward progress. Some systems will develop into storms with winds of up to 120 km/h (74 mph). Any faster than that, and the storm becomes a hurricane. The strongest storms— category 5 hurricanes— have winds of more than 250 km/h (157 mph).

What is a hurricane?

A better view of the huge storms slowly emerged. Sakuhei Fujiwhara, a Japanese researcher (see box, left) showed how hurricanes fitted into the bigger weather picture of the tropical Atlantic. In 1922 Edward Bowie found that hurricanes generally rotate anti-cyclonically, or opposite to the direction of Earth's rotation. In the Northern Hemisphere that would be counterclockwise. However, these details were not helping the warning centers get the message out early enough, and hurricanes hitting the coast would frequently result in hundreds of deaths.

By the late 1940s, some big pieces of the puzzle were falling into place, thanks mostly to pilots flying aircraft into hurricanes to plot wind speeds and pressure changes, and map out the mysterious eye, a place of calm at the very center of the storm. In 1948, the Finnish meteorologist Erik Palmén showed that a hurricane requires surface water temperatures of at least 26°C (80°F) in order to form. The water needs to be at least 50 m (160 ft) deep, too. The air above this warm sea churns with the heat. As the air rises it cools down faster than normal, making the water vapor condense into thick clouds. The latent heat of this condensation adds energy to the system, pulling more and more air and water up from the surface. The upward flow of the air creates the beginnings of a central eye, and cooler air from far above falls into it, reducing the air pressure at the heart of the system even further, pulling in more air moisture to create an expanding area. This process will continue until the storm hits land or moves into cooler seas.

WEATHER SATELLITES

It is hard to comprehend just how large a hurricane is. Trying to capture a picture of one required the development of space technology. The first weather satellite, Vanguard 2, was launched in 1959. It used a primitive digital camera to take pictures of cloud cover. The results were fuzzy and not very useful. However, U.S. earth scientists persevered with this space system, and since the late 1970s, two GOES (Geostationary Operational Environmental Satellites) have offered a big picture view of the whole of Earth (and its hurricanes).

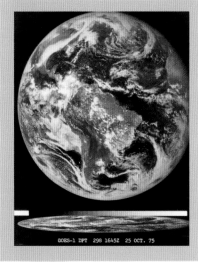

56 Challenger Expedition

CAN YOU GUESS WHAT THE SCIENCE OF OCEANOGRAPHY STUDIES? IT'S NOT A DIFFICULT QUESTION, perhaps because this is a young science that has its origins in the voyage of HMS *Challenger*, a British navy ship kitted out as the first ocean science ship in 1872.

Upon its return in 1876, having sailed 130,000 km (81,000 miles), *Challenger* had made a great wealth of discoveries. The expedition was the brainchild of Charles Wyville Thomson, a Scottish zoologist. He suggested a mission to map the great oceanic basins of Earth and make a global survey of the salt content and turbidity (or clarity) of ocean water. He petitioned the Royal Society of London to take the lead. HMS *Challenger* was made ready by converting her from a fighting ship to a science vessel, packed with instruments, nets, and sampling equipment and complete with its own chemistry lab. *Challenger* had a steam engine, which could power the vessel but was mostly used to drive a dredge for scooping up sediments.

About 240 crew set sail on HMS Challenger, *and 144 came home. Some of the missing had died, while others deserted.*

The plan was to circumnavigate Earth, but the route was somewhat circuitous as it toured all major ocean basins. The expedition made its most lasting discovery on arrival in the Western Pacific. The crew took 360 depth soundings in total, and the deepest was between the islands of Guam and Palau, where the seabed was 8,184 m (26,850 feet) down. This region, part of the Marianas Trench, is today called Challenger Deep. The latest survey from 2011 revealed that the deepest point there (and anywhere on Earth) is actually 10,994 m (36,070 ft), which is easily deep enough to submerge Mount Everest.

Below: A map of the oceans made by the Challenger Expedition indicates surface water density. Yellow is the highest density and pink is the lowest.

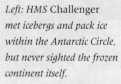

Left: HMS Challenger *met icebergs and pack ice within the Antarctic Circle, but never sighted the frozen continent itself.*

57 USGS

DURING THE 19TH CENTURY, THE UNITED STATES WAS GROWING RAPIDLY WESTWARD, AND SETTLERS WERE ARRIVING to set up home on parcels of land provided by the government. However, by the 1870s the system of land management was getting out of control.

A copy of the law establishing the U.S. Geological Survey in 1879.

During the confederation of the United States in the 1780s, it was agreed that the land west of the Allegheny Mountains should be under the control of the U.S. Congress. This was partly to avoid quarrels between the states, and also so that the federal government could sell land to boost revenue and encourage settlers to move into this new territory. However, a third of all mineral wealth was to be retained for the nation. These same rules applied as the United States expanded all the way to the Pacific, acquiring new territory from other nations or taking it from the native residents. Very little was known about the Wild West, and it was the job of local surveyors to declare if the federal government had any claim on a plot of land—a system wide open to corruption. There were several serious attempts to map the West, but they were led by private explorers or individual states, and so lacked coordination. Therefore, on March 3, 1879, just a few hours before the 45th Congress closed for elections, President Rutherford B. Hayes created the Geological Survey. Its job was "classification of the public lands, and examination of the geological structure, mineral resources, and products of the national domain."

Public mission

In the early days, the survey designated all U.S. territory as eight types of land. It was looking for lead, copper, and precious metals, plus other minerals like coal and iron that were not listed as significant in the original land rulings a century before. Today, that task of surveying is over, but the USGS has several important jobs to fulfill including planning for earthquake and volcano hazards, mapping land and water use, monitoring any effects of extreme weather, and watching for diseases spreading through U.S.wildlife. Finally, USGS staff help space scientists develop systems for exploring other worlds.

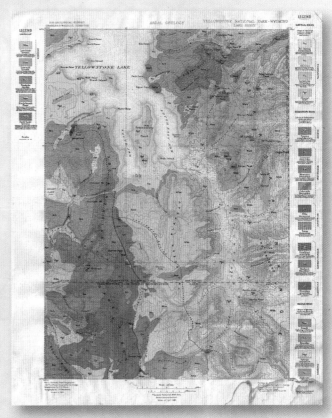

This map of part of Yellowstone National Park showing hot springs, rivers and creeks, marshes, geysers, lakes, and ponds, was published by the U.S. Geological Survey in 1884.

58 Cumulonimbus

IN 1880, A NEW KIND OF CLOUD WAS ADDED TO THE LIST, THE CUMULONIMBUS. This makes an imposing sight, one that is worth our attention because it is the main source of thunder, lightning, and tornadoes.

Philip Weilbach was an art historian and the librarian at Copenhagen's Art Academy, and so was an unexpected figure in the world of cloud classification. In 1880 he presented his descriptions of clouds to the International Meteorological Organization (IMO), but the IMO's committee did not accept most of them, feeling that they were too different from the system (now widely in use) devised by Luke Howard at the start of the century. However, one of Weilbach's proposals did add something to the understanding of clouds. He described a vertical rain cloud, which he called a cumulonimbus (meaning "heaped rain cloud"). This cloud often had cirrus formations at the top and was able to produce thunder. The IMO liked his description and chose to eject Howard's cumulostratus from the classification as a poorly described version of the same cloud type.

Cumulonimbus can form alone, in clusters, or along cold fronts. They grow from overdeveloped cumulus clouds and may further develop as part of a super cell, such as is shown above, which can spawn tornadoes.

NOCTILUCENT CLOUDS

This rare kind of cloud—it's name means "night glowing"—is only seen in the twilight of short summer nights. While other clouds are always below a height of 14 km (45,000 feet), noctilucents are clouds of ice crystals 80 km (50 miles) up. How they form in this dry part of the atmosphere is a mystery.

Thunderhead

A cumulonimbus is a towering, vertical rain cloud that can reach 12,000 meters (39,000 ft) tall. It forms from powerful updrafts above warm land that lift moisture high into the air. Frequently this moisture falls back down again as heavy rain. During a storm, these clouds are called thunderheads. Friction between sections of the cloud creates an electrical potential. Eventually this will discharge to the ground or between the clouds as lightning. The lightning bolt heats the air, making it expand rapidly and produce a shock wave that is heard as a clap of thunder.

59 The Krakatoa Eruption

AT 10.02 A.M. ON AUGUST 27, 1883, A VOLCANO ON A SMALL ISLAND WEST OF JAVA EXPLODED, MAKING THE LOUDEST NOISE IN RECORDED HISTORY. The resulting tsunami was detected as far away as England.

The volcano, Krakatoa, had started erupting the day before, churning out a huge ash cloud. Two smaller explosions had preceded the big one in the late morning. That was heard 3,110 km (1,930 miles) away in Perth, Australia, and on Rodrigues Island in the Indian Ocean 4,800 km (3,000 miles) in the opposite direction. All three explosions produced tsunamis that reached more than 30 meters (98 feet) high when they made landfall. These waves were the deadliest aspects of the eruption, and at least 36,417 people were killed on land and at sea by the eruption.

The Krakatoa blast was four times more powerful than even the largest thermonuclear bombs ever tested. It turned the 790-m (2,600-foot) mountain into a 6.5-km (4-mile) wide crater, or caldera, created by a magma chamber beneath the seabed collapsing and filling with seawater. The mountain became 21 cubic km (5 cubic miles) of dust and ash. The cloud blocked out the Sun for three days and darkened the atmosphere enough to reduce global temperatures for five years.

EAST OF JAVA?

In 1969 a Hollywood disaster movie starring Maximilian Schell recreated the events of the 1883 eruption. It won a nomination for the Academy Award for Best Visual Effects. The characters are engaged in the recovery of a cargo of pearls from a shipwreck close to the volcano. The studio wanted an exotic title and opted for *Krakatoa, East of Java*. Producers were unconcerned that the mountain was actually west of Java. A re-released cut was titled simply *Volcano*.

The island of Krakatoa appears tranquil before the eruption that wiped it from the map in 1883.

60 Mountain Building

BY THE 1880S IT WAS WIDELY AGREED THAT MOUNTAINS WERE BEING GRADUALLY WORN AWAY BY EROSION, so even the mightiest ranges of today would become small hills in the distant future. But what pushed mountains up in the first place?

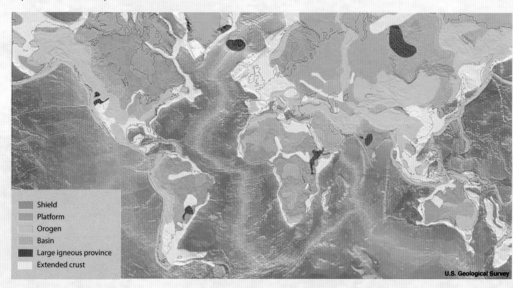

Left: The cyan-colored regions of this world map show the "orogenic belts," or regions which are being thrust upward into mountains.

Shield
Platform
Orogen
Basin
Large igneous province
Extended crust

U.S. Geological Survey

James Dwight Dana, the American mineralogist (see page 62) was an advocate of the contracting Earth theory. This suggested that Earth had begun as a molten ball of rock. A solid crust had formed as the planet cooled. However, cooling further made the rock contract and this made the crust crack. The cracks were seen on the surface as large-scale features, including mountain ranges. However, by the mid-1880s, evidence collected by multiple teams of researchers in the Alps, Scottish Highlands, and the Rockies suggested something different. Faults or cracks running down through rock strata allowed for older rock layers to be pushed up and over younger ones.

Below: Thrust forces result at first in a bulging "ramp anticline." Then the strata begin to break up, creating a more complex landscape.

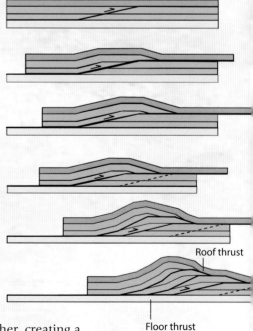

Roof thrust

Floor thrust

Up and over

These features were called thrust faults, and the way they arise—thrust fault theory—forms the basis for a new way of understanding orogeny, the process that builds mountain ranges. The theory explains that when a region of rock is being compressed laterally, the fault allows one side to slide up the other, creating a thicker region of rock. When entire continents push against each other, the result is a mountain range soaring far above sea level. The study of thrust faults on a small scale gave an indication of the processes that shaped the planet on the largest scale.

61 El Niño

PERUVIAN SAILORS TOLD OF A WARM CURRENT THAT FLOWED SOUTH SOME YEARS AROUND CHRISTMAS TIME. They called it El Niño (The Little Boy), referring to the baby Jesus, and today it is known to be a global weather event.

Camilo Carrillo Martinez had an illustrious naval career before becoming the finance minister of Peru in the 1870s.

The first official account of "El Niño" with reference to the climate was made by Captain Camilo Carrillo Martinez when he explained the old sailors' lore to the geographical society in Lima in 1892. Today we know that El Niño is the warm phase of an ocean system called the El Niño–Southern Oscillation (ENSO). It arises when a mass of warmer water develops in the equatorial region of the central Pacific Ocean (generally somewhere between approximately 180°, the International Date Line, and 120° W). That brings the water up to the west coast of South America toward the end of the year—El Niño has arrived. However, the ENSO is not an annual event, but a multi-year cycle between warm and cold sea surface temperature. In some years the water is much colder, a phase that is dubbed La Niña (see box, below).

In an El Niño year, warm ocean water builds up along the western coast of South America, which normally experiences a cold current. This shift is part of a cycle of climatic effects that has an impact on the whole Pacific region—and even further afield.

Climate effects

El Niño brings high air pressure and drought to the west of the Pacific Ocean, and low pressure and heavy rains to the eastern side. On average there are four years between each El Niño, although some cycles can run for around seven years. The impact of ENSO is significant on agricultural output in the Pacific region as temperature and rainfall vary considerably at different points in the cycle. The effects felt by today's changing climate include increases in the temperature difference between the warm and cool phases, and may result in more extreme weather effects, such as droughts.

LA NIÑA

The cold phase of the El Niño–Southern Oscillation is called La Niña, which means "little girl" to indicate it is the opposite part of the cycle to El Niño. In this phase, the surface of the eastern and central Pacific become colder due to water upwelling from deeper down, so the warmer waters move to the western Pacific for a few years. La Niña periods are cold but dry in South America and wetter over in the western Pacific. To continue the cycle, cold water streams west at the surface, and the warmer water moves eastward deeper down before rising to the surface near Peru, bringing El Niño back.

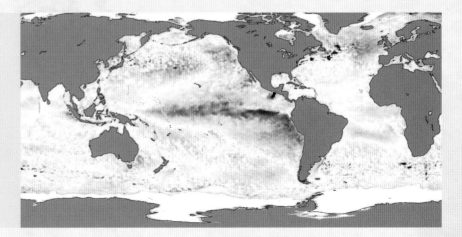

62 Greenhouse Effect

IN 1896, THE SWEDISH CHEMIST SVANTE ARRHENIUS GAVE THE FIRST FULL DESCRIPTION OF WHAT WE NOW KNOW AS THE GREENHOUSE EFFECT. His interest in it came from his theory of how Earth could cool down to create ice ages, and today the phenomenon helps us understand climate.

The greenhouse effect is an entirely natural phenomenon that allows Earth's atmosphere to trap some of the solar energy that arrives from space. That keeps the planet's average temperature at a tolerable 14° C (57° F)—you'd still better bring a coat. Without the effect, the surface of the planet would be an icy –18°C (0° F). During the 19th century the existence and mechanism of the greenhouse effect were revealed, including Arrhenius's exposition on its impact on climate change in the long term. In more recent years the phrase "greenhouse effect" has become jumbled during the debates, both scientific and political, about the impact that human changes to the atmosphere are having on our climate—this time in the short term.

A new idea

The idea of a greenhouse effect was proposed by the French mathematician Joseph Fourier in 1824. In 1856 the American Eunice Newton Foote provided experimental evidence of the differing thermal properties of atmospheric gases. Carbon dioxide, she discovered, became much hotter when exposed to sunlight than oxygen and nitrogen. A few years later, the Irish physicist John Tyndall became famous for doing much the same experiment and also measured how different gases radiated their heat away.

Like in a greenhouse, visible wavelengths of sunlight can get into Earth's atmosphere, but not all the invisible heat energy can get out again. The net result is a warming of the planet.

FOSSIL FUELS

Plant life "fixes" carbon dioxide gas and uses it as a raw material for growth. Animals eat plants, using oxygen to burn this food and release energy. Waste carbon dioxide is released back into the air. This cycle is self-limiting. However fossil fuels, like oil, gas, and coal, are the carbon-rich remains of ancient life. When burnt, their carbon dioxide released into the air is not part of the natural carbon cycle, and so it continues to build up in the air.

Right: Svante Arrhenius's paper, On the Influence of Carbonic Acid in the Air upon the Temperature of the Ground *has certainly left its mark on the world.*

THE
LONDON, EDINBURGH, AND DUBLIN
PHILOSOPHICAL MAGAZINE
AND
JOURNAL OF SCIENCE.

[FIFTH SERIES.]

APRIL 1896.

XXXI. *On the Influence of Carbonic Acid in the Air upon the Temperature of the Ground.* By Prof. SVANTE ARRHENIUS*.

Currently, the land and oceans are able to absorb half of the excess carbon dioxide released by humans. If in future that rate of absorption drops, then more carbon dioxide (and the extra heat) will gather in the atmosphere. Using data from its latest carbon-dioxide mapping satellite, NASA produced this map of the Earth showing high concentrations (red) and low (blue) if the rate of absortion should drop by half. It suggests that the frozen north will heat up much more than everywhere else.

He did not credit the contribution of Foote. Nevertheless it was Arrhenius, an expert on how chemicals absorb and give out energy, who set out the impact on climate. Our atmosphere is largely transparent; light shines straight through (although blue rays are scattered, which is why the sky appears blue). Sunlight warms the Earth's surface, which radiates the energy back into space as invisible heat radiation. Oxygen, nitrogen, and argon, which together make up more than 99 percent of the air, let this heat pass through unaffected. However, carbon dioxide (just 0.04 percent of the atmosphere) and other greenhouse gases, such as methane and water vapor, absorb heat and warm up the atmosphere. Gardeners will know that the glass of a greenhouse does the same, letting light in but stopping heat from getting out. Nils Gustaf Ekholm obviously did know, because he coined the term "greenhouse effect" in 1902.

Climate change

Carbon dioxide is released into the atmosphere as a waste product of life. Gasp! You breathe it out. Arrhenius correlated temperature changes with shifts in the amount of carbon dioxide in the air. He wondered if sudden falls in carbon dioxide caused ice ages. But a rise would change climate, too. Even in Arrhenius's day, growing industrial concerns relied on using fossil fuels as a source of energy. It was assumed that the carbon dioxide they released was simply absorbed by plants and the ocean, but by the end of the 1950s, it was clear that carbon dioxide levels in the air were rising (and still are). Arrhenius's math is unequivocal—that means the air is also getting warmer, slowly but surely. Extreme weather is the symptom and result of a climate that is changing. Sea level rise or fall is related to how much ice freezes around the poles, and all of this can be traced to changes in the amount of greenhouse gases.

RUNAWAY PLANET

Our nearest neighbor in space, the planet Venus, has an atmospheric greenhouse effect as well, only much more extreme. The planet's surface, seen here in a radar scan, is hidden by a thick, foggy atmosphere composed mostly of carbon dioxide. The greenhouse effect makes Venus the hottest planet of all, with a surface temperature of 462° C (864° F), and an atmospheric pressure 90 times higher than that on Earth.

63 Exploring Antarctica

IT USED TO BE THOUGHT THAT MOST OF THE SOUTHERN HEMISPHERE WAS FILLED WITH A VAST CONTINENT. However, successive explorers found little but treacherous ocean, icebergs, and sheets of ice. That led to an indifference to the region, and it would take heroic efforts to find out more.

In 1837, French ships commanded by Jules Dumont d'Urville got the first glimpse of the coast of Antarctica (a landmass mostly buried under a thick ice sheet). A few years later a British expedition led by James Clark Ross dismissed the territory as not being worth the risk of exploring. It was more than 50 years before explorers returned in earnest, in what has since been described as the Heroic Age of Antarctic Exploration. This was characterized by teams braving terrible conditions to open up the icy continent to scrutiny—and frequently dying in the process. The first attempt was a Belgian expedition in 1897, which was the first to experience the Antarctic winter (having got stuck in sea ice). The following year the British Southern Cross Expedition made it to the mainland. As well as surveying the coast and wildlife (mainly seals and penguins), successive expeditions tried to reach "Farthest South," each time getting a little closer to the South Pole. This competition ended in January 1912, when Robert Scott, an English explorer, reached the pole, only to find that Roald Amundsen, (a Norwegian who had been first mate on that first Belgian mission) had got there the month before.

The Southern Cross Expedition from 1898 to 1900 was the first earth science mission to the continental landmass of Antarctica. There has been permanent human settlement in Antarctica since 1956, and in 1978, the first Antarctican baby was born in an Argentine base.

MECHANICAL AGE

In the 1920s the Heroic Age of Antarctic Exploration gave way to the Mechanical Age. Today around 4,000 people, almost entirely earth scientists of one stripe or another, live in Antarctica during the summer. (Several bases have their own ice runways for transport aircraft.) In winter, the population drops to around 1,000. The ice slowly buries Antarctica's buildings. For example, the British Halley Research Station has been replaced six times in 65 years. The latest base (above) walks on hydraulic legs so it can climb out of accumulating snow—and move to a better location.

64 Weather Balloons

THE ANTICS OF COXWELL AND GLAISHER HAD SHOWN THAT IT WAS IMPOSSIBLE FOR SCIENTISTS to gather data from high altitude. So automatic instruments were sent up by balloon.

Just as oceanographers used remote devices to plumb the depths and record conditions in the deep ocean, "aerologists," who studied the atmosphere, had to figure out how to get their instruments high into the sky. The first attempts used kites to lift meteographs, which were recording devices that measured air pressure and temperature. A kite is always tethered to the ground, so any data was extracted from the device on landing. But flying such a setup to any appreciable height was extremely difficult.

In 1892, Frenchmen Gustave Hermite and Georges Besançon developed an unmanned weather balloon system that solved the altitude problem. They used paper hydrogen balloons that were capable of carrying around 10 kg (22 lbs) of instrumentation to above 10 km (6 miles). They later updated these to rubber balloons that expanded with altitude and reached even greater heights. The balloons would burst when the difference in pressure between the gas inside and the thinning air outside became too great. But how to get at the data collected? The solution was to fix parachutes to the meteographs, which would then float safely back to the ground.

Mass ascent

In 1896 the French meteorologist Léon Philippe Teisserenc de Bort began conducting experiments into clouds and the high atmosphere using hydrogen balloons. He found that the air temperature decreased steadily with height, but at about 11,000 m (36,000 ft) the temperature leveled off. And it stayed more or less constant, even as the pressure dropped further with altitude—or at least he was unable to get his balloons high enough to detect any further changes in temperature. Over about five years, Teisserenc de Bort launched more than 200 balloons, often at night to remove the effects of solar heating. Finally he was confident in his discovery: the atmosphere was made of two layers. He named the lower one the "troposphere," which relates to its changing conditions. All weather is made from churning air masses in this layer. The next layer was the "stratosphere" in reference to its layers of constant temperature. Today, we know that there are three more layers higher still (see box, left).

ATMOSPHERIC LAYERS

Earth's atmosphere is divided into five layers. Nearest the surface is the troposphere, the location of weather systems. The stratosphere is made of air that gets warmer with height. Temperature drops again in the mesosphere, which is the coldest part of Earth's system, going as low as −113° C (−171° F). The thermosphere steadily thins out as the air fades into outer space (spacecraft often orbit here), while the exosphere contains traces of gases held in Earth's gravitational field.

EXOSPHERE

600 km
(375 miles)

THERMOSPHERE

120 km
(75 miles)

MESOSPHERE

60km
(35 miles)

STRATOSPHERE
11km
(7 miles)
TROPOSPHERE

RADIOSONDE

Weather balloons are still a cheap and effective tool for meteorologists. Today they carry a radiosonde (the above example dates from 1936), which is a battery-powered instrument that transmits any data it collects in real time down to the ground by radio. As well as temperature, pressure, and altitude, radiosondes detect wind and air chemistry. A dropsonde is a similar device deployed from an aircraft and goes to work as it falls earthward.

65 Earth's Heat

ANCIENT THOUGHT DICTATED THAT EARTH WAS THE SOURCE OF COLD. THE EVIDENCE? ROCK IS COLD TO THE TOUCH. However, better evidence abounded that this was manifestly false, not least from volcanic eruptions and hot springs: Earth is hot inside. Where does that heat come from?

In 1862 William Thomson, better known today as Lord Kelvin, decided to following the example of the Comte de Buffon almost a century before. Being an authority on thermodynamics—it was he who calculated absolute zero—Kelvin meticulously calculated how long it would take for an Earth-sized ball of molten rock to cool into a planet with a solid surface with the same average temperature of Earth. He alighted at a maximum figure of 400 million years. Immediately everyone saw the problem. Geologists, who went by the principle of uniformitarianism, or that "the present is the key to the past," were studying the process of how rocks formed from layers of fragments that covered the surface of Earth. One thing was certain, it was a slow process and 400 million years was just not long enough to fit in all the rock building, rock bending, and rock erosion required to make a planet that looked like Earth. The biologists agreed. They needed much longer for evolution by natural selection (a hot new topic) to diversify life on Earth. The clamor of opposition to the eminent physicist's conclusions grew. His assumptions had to be wrong.

George Darwin, the son of Charles, was one of the first scientists to suggest that Earth was heated internally by radioactive decay.

Slow chill or extra heat

One obvious suggestion was that the planet was not a uniform material. Perhaps the flow of heat from inside Earth was slowed by some as yet unknown structure. (If anything, our understanding of Earth's interior shows that it contains vast convective plumes, which would dissipate heat faster than the theoretical system used by Kelvin in his calculations.) The only other possibility is that as well as the primordial heat left over from the formation of Earth, our planet has its own supply of heat, produced by the decay of radioactive elements in its interior. Radioactivity was not discovered until 1895, but within a decade it was put forward by George Darwin (son of Charles) as a solution to the problem of Earth's "heat budget." The field of radioactivity would, in the end, solve the confusion of Earth's true age through radiometric dating (see page 83).

TIDAL MOON THEORY

The astronomer George Darwin initially provided corroboration of Lord Kelvin's estimate of the Earth's age. Darwin theorized that the Moon (below) was caused by centrifugal forces within the young Earth (still molten), which resulted in a chunk of material being flung into orbit. This cooled into today's Moon, Darwin explained. The Moon's rotation is tidally locked to Earth's (that's why we always see one side). Darwin calculated it would take 56 million years for this locked state to arise.

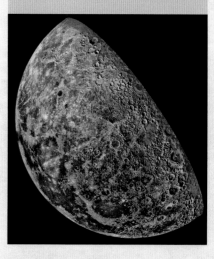

(see page 83)

66 The Moho

ANCIENT PEOPLE HAD LONG KNOWN THAT TREMORS IN THE GROUND WERE A SIGN OF WORSE TO COME. However, by the mid-19th century, a new science, seismology, began to use waves, such as those that cause earthquakes, as a way to see inside Earth.

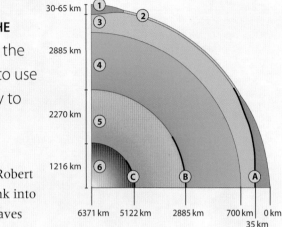

The term *seismology* was coined in 1857 by the Irish geologist Robert Mallet. He created his own seismic waves using explosives sunk into the ground to help him develop machines to detect natural waves and to learn how the waves moved through different rocks. In 1897, Emil Wiechert, an experimental physicist, briefly turned into a theoretical geophysicist. He compared the overall density of Earth with the average density of rocks at the surface—which was lower—and theorized the difference must mean Earth's interior is made of two layers, an iron core and a surrounding coating or mantle of rock-like, silicate minerals. This was backed up with evidence in 1906 when Richard Dixon Oldham showed seismic waves were being blocked or deflected by a dense core.

Wave types

Seismology is based on the fact that seismic waves are reflected or refracted in a similar way to light waves or ripples on a pond. Seismographs all over the world pick up what waves hit the surface where, and that builds up a picture of the paths they take and the materials they come across deep inside the planet. In 1909 the Croatian Andrija Mohorovičić saw that waves habitually changed speed at around 20 km (10 miles) under continents and 5 km (3 miles) under the ocean floor. Above this point the waves were moving through solid rock; below was something denser. This boundary has become known as the Mohorovičić discontinuity—Moho for short—and it shows where Earth's mantle changes into a thin, third, and outer layer, called the crust.

Today, there are three discontinuities known inside Earth. The Moho discontinuity (A) separates thick continental crust (1) and thinner oceanic crust (2) from the upper mantle (3). The Gutenberg discontinuity (B) separates the lower mantle (4) from the molten outer core (5), while the Lehmann–Bullen discontinuity (C) marks the outer edge of the solid inner core (6).

THE FIRST SEISMOGRAPH

In 132 CE, the Chinese engineer Zhang Heng invented the "earthquake weathervane." It was a bronze urn with a pendulum inside. When this swung due to movement of the ground it dislodged one of eight balls held in dragon heads equally spaced around the device. The dropped ball fell into a waiting toad's mouth, and indicated the direction from which the tremor arrived.

67 The Cambrian Explosion

A WEALTH OF FOSSILS FOUND LOCKED AWAY IN SHALE ROCKS IN THE **C**ANADIAN **R**OCKIES revealed that Earth's complex lifeforms—the kinds of which we still see today—exploded into history around 500 million years ago.

MAOTIANSHAN SHALES

This rock formation in China is very similar to that found in the Rockies, except it is 10 million years older. When excavated in the 1980s, the Maotianshan Shales revealed a similar set of fossils to its Canadian counterpart, including *Jianfengia* (above), an arthropod predator that hunted with tough appendages on its head. The Chinese fossils showed that the diversification of life on Earth was already well under way 520 million years ago.

The rock formation was called the Burgess Shale. It had been scouted out as a rich source of fossils in the late 1890s, but the true treasure trove was revealed in 1910 by Charles Doolittle Walcott, an American paleontologist, who had only recently stepped down from running the USGS. The fossil hunt became a family affair, with Charles's sons and daughter camping out in the mountains for extended field trips. His second wife Helena died in 1911, but by 1914 Charles had remarried Mary Vaux, who was a celebrated nature artist and a useful addition to the team. By 1924, Team Walcott had dug up 65,000 specimens, all from an ancient seabed and all Cambrian in age. The Cambrian, named for rocks originally found in Wales, is the first period in the Paleozoic Era. Its rocks are the first to have fossils—at least that was the belief at the time. In Walcott's day, the age of those rocks was a matter of guesswork, but today Cambrian rocks are dated between 541 and 485 million years old. The Burgess Shale rocks are 508 million years old.

Charles Doolittle Walcott takes a break from fossil hunting at the Burgess Shale, and, to his left, an illustration of a brachiopod fossil, a kind of shellfish that once abounded in Cambrian seas but is much rarer now.

All life is here

Walcott was ultimately defeated by the scale of the task, and it was not until the 1960s that a coherent analysis was made of his fossils that were gathering dust at the Smithsonian Institution. The conclusion was that almost every phylum (major grouping) of animal that is alive today was represented in the fossils. That includes arthropods, like insects and spiders, worms galore, jellyfish, and even a tiny, fish-like creature. The fossil record goes from no apparent life to all this diversity in a few million years, an event that is called the Cambrian Explosion.

68 Radiometric Dating

IN THE EARLY YEARS OF THE 20TH CENTURY, DISCOVERIES ABOUT RADIOACTIVITY OPENED UP THE OPPORTUNITY to date rocks using their atoms. What would this new technique reveal about the age of Earth?

In the early 1900s, a pair of physicists, Ernest Rutherford and Frederick Soddy, showed that radioactivity was all about unstable atoms falling apart, releasing energy and material, and transforming into new kinds of elements. (Remember, an element is a substance with a specific atomic structure. Radioactivity changes atomic structure, so one element is converted into another.) Rutherford and Soddy showed that it is impossible to predict the radioactive decay of individual atoms, but they did follow a half-life pattern, which means that the time it takes for half of a quantity of radioactive material to decay away is a constant. Today we know of highly unstable radioactive substances that have a half-life lasting millionths of a second, although the most common radioactive elements in rocks, thorium and uranium, have half-lives measured in millions of years. If you know the primordial quantity of these metals—the amount that existed when the rock formed—then the amount present today would tell you how old the rock is.

Arthur Holmes showed that the amount of radioactive material in rocks was lower in older specimens.

RADIOCARBON DATING

Cosmic rays smashing into nitrogen in the high atmosphere create a radioactive form of carbon—C-14. All living things have a tiny amount of C-14 in them, kept replenished throughout life. Once the organism dies, the C-14 begins to decay away. Any remains of living things—cotton, hair, bones, or wood—can be dated by the amount of C-14. The system works for anything up to 50,000 years old, such as fossil humans, and artifacts, such as this 400-year-old Chinese wooden carving.

Into action

Several researchers tried to measure radioactive decay by the quantity of alpha particles present. These are small, charged particles that are flung out of atoms during decay. However, a simpler approach is to make use of what is called the decay chain. Radioactive uranium, for example, will decay into several highly unstable atoms, including things like radon, radium, and polonium, before arriving at a stable form of lead. The American chemist Bertram Boltwood pioneered this approach by comparing the proportions of uranium and lead in rocks to measure their age, and proposed some of them were 500 million years old. In 1911, the British researcher Arthur Holmes found rocks that were 1.6 billion years old. He refined that up to 3 billion years in 1927. In the 1950s, a better understanding of radioactive decay chains led to scientists dating meteorites at 4.55 billion years old: that is the age of Earth and the Solar System.

Zircon minerals are the oldest objects on Earth. Some crystals are more than 4 billion years old.

69 Continental Drift

WHEN THE FIRST ACCURATE WORLD MAPS BECAME WIDELY AVAILABLE, MANY PEOPLE NOTICED THE SAME THING: it looks like the world's land would all fit together like a jigsaw puzzle. That was the start of a very big idea.

The first world maps that bore a true likeness of the Earth's landmasses appeared in the late 16th century (see box, below). Even so, many features of those maps were still based on guesswork and wishful thinking—especially in the Arctic and Antarctic, and the eastern coast of the Pacific Ocean was barely explored by Europeans. However, the Atlantic Ocean and its coasts had been well surveyed. Straight away—from Abraham Ortelius, the publisher of the very first atlas, onward—people started to wonder why it was that the Atlantic coast of South America appeared to fit so snugly with its counterpart over in Africa. Abraham Ortelius even suggested that the Americas were "torn away from Europe and Africa … by earthquakes and floods. The vestiges of the rupture reveal themselves if someone brings forward a map of the world and considers carefully the coasts."

Alexander von Humboldt had a similar view more than a century later. Around the same time, Charles Lyell, who had done much to make geology a mainstream science in the 1830s, summed up a general view: "Continents, therefore, although permanent for whole geological epochs, shift their positions entirely in the course of ages."

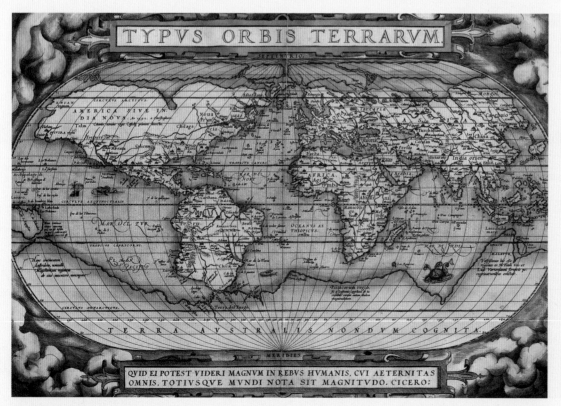

THEATER OF THE WORLD

Regarded as the first world atlas, this book was published in Belgium by the geographer Abraham Ortelius in 1570, under the name *Theatrum orbis terrarum*. Ortelius wrote descriptions of the lands on display but only created a few of the maps himself. Instead, the book was a collection of 53 maps drawn by other master cartographers, arranged in continents. The map still included a vast, mostly speculative *Terra Australis* in place of Antarctica. Interestingly, this continent was shown swinging north between the Indian Ocean and the Pacific to cover where Australia is. So, nearly 40 years before that island continent became known to Europeans in the 1600s, the collective knowledge of cartographers already suggested that there was something there.

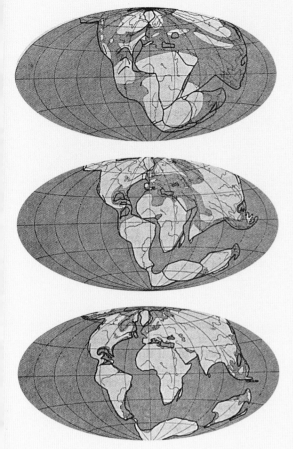

Drawings made by Alfred Wegener sketch out how today's continents were once connected in a single landmass (Pangaea, meaning "whole Earth"), and then drifted apart to make today's world map.

Permanence

However, a new breed of 19th-century geologists balked at the idea of an ever-changing surface to the planet. (Just imagine how long it would all take!) A chief proponent of a fixed geography was James Dana, who followed up his *Manual of Mineralogy* with a *Manual of Geology* in 1863. In that book he declared: "The continents and oceans had their general outline or form defined in earliest time." This view became known as permanence theory, and with Dana's academic weight behind it, it was hard to shift. The best evidence for permanence was the continental shelf, which appeared to be built from sediments washed off the land by rivers. If continents were on the move, why did these considerable underwater features exist?

Getting the drift

The older idea that the Atlantic Ocean formed when the Americas split from Africa and Asia—and by the same token, all the world's continents are slowly shifting and reshaping—now has a name to compete with permanence theory: continental drift. That is attributed to the German meteorologist Alfred Wegener, who coined it (at least a German version) in 1912. In the following years, he promoted the idea with evidence from corresponding fossil records and matching geological strata that pointed to the fact that at some point in the distant past, all the world's current seven continents had once been joined. Any differences in fossils and strata between continents date from those splits. Wegener named the single supercontinent Pangaea and surrounded it with Panthalassa, a single superocean. This chimed with earlier ideas from Eduard Suess, who used the same reasoning to propose a southern supercontinent called Gondwana divided from a northern one, Laurasia, by the Tethys Ocean. Both men were right: Pangaea split into Gondwana and Laurasia about 200 million years ago. However, the question was: how did solid land drift? Wegener suggested it was the centrifugal forces of Earth's spin that forced land through the sea-floor. The truth, uncovered in the 1960s, would be more revealing of how the world really works.

Alfred Wegener, left, with Greenlandic explorer Rasmus Villumsen, during an expedition to central Greenland in 1930. Both men were dead within a month of this photograph being taken, killed by the Arctic winter.

70 Metamorphic Rock

IN 1912, A BRITISH GEOLOGIST IDENTIFIED A NEW TYPE OF ROCK IN EARTH'S CRUST:
metamorphic rocks. This introduced a third process in the rock cycle, where
high pressures and temperatures transform the composition of solid rocks.

The geologist responsible
was George Barrow, a
bright and able Londoner
who had excelled at
mathematics and the
sciences. Choosing to
specialize in geology,
Barrow began to map the
stratigraphy of the Scottish
Highlands in the 1890s.
After 20 years of careful
work, he presented what is
now known, in his honor,
as a Barrovian gradient.
Barrow's map showed that
the rocks could be divided
into distinct layers according to the arrival of specific minerals. In the ensuing decade,
the Finnish geologist Pentti Eskola, explained why.

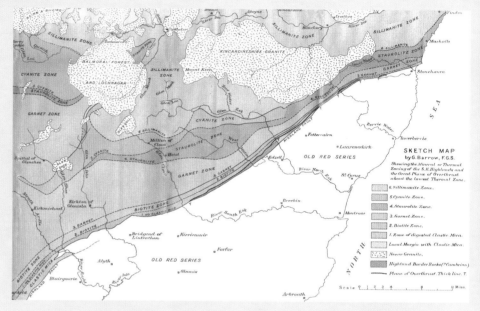

*A map by George Barrow,
published in 1912, showing
what became known as the
Highland Boundary Fault.*

*The process of
metamorphism makes
minerals in rocks line up
into sheets, a phenomenon
called foliation. The degree
of foliation goes some way
to revealing the grade
of metamorphism, or
how much pressure and
temperature were applied.*

Metamorphism

The Barrovian gradient was the simplest form of a metamorphic change, which
involves both pressure and temperature increasing with depth. These changing factors
create physical and chemical changes in the minerals that made up the original rock

(the protolith). If the minerals change, the rock changes, and the end result is a range of new rock types that vary according to the forces that made them. Barrovian gradients are typical of mountain-building zones, where rocks are squeezed deep beneath the Earth. Other metamorphic zones are close to magma chambers and volcanic fissures, where heat rather than pressure dominates. In addition, meteorite impacts can create small pockets of metamorphic rocks. Igneous and sedimentary rocks all have associated metamorphs. For example, limestones become marble, shales become slate, and sandstones make quartzite. Other metamorphic rocks, such as schists and gneiss, have a more generic origin.

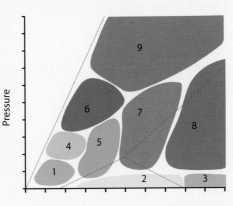

METAMORPHIC FACIES

In 1921, the Finnish geologist Pentti Eskola described zones called metamorphic facies, where different combinations of pressure and temperature produce a particular set of minerals. These then combine into metamorphic rock. The facies are: 1) zeolite; 2) hornfels; 3) sanidinite; 4) prehnite-pumpellyite; 5) greenschist; 6) blueschist; 7) amphibolite; 8) granulite; 9) eclogite.

71 Dendrochronology

TREES ADD A NEW LAYER OF WOOD EVERY YEAR, creating the familiar concentric rings. As well as being a good way of figuring out how old a tree is, tree ring data is also valuable in climate research.

Dendrochronology (*dendron* is Greek for "tree") is the idea of counting rings in a trunk to figure out how old the tree is. It was first recorded by Leonardo da Vinci. He knew that in summer, the tree grew faster, leaving a band of paler, softer wood. In winter, growth slowed, leaving a narrow, dark band. Together, these rings account for one year, and big tree trunks have hundreds of them. Da Vinci even knew that a cold year created distinctive darker rings, so the trunk acted as a record of past climate. This simple but effective idea was toyed with over the centuries but with little purpose. Then in 1920, the American astronomer A. E. Douglass found a reason to formalize the process. He wanted to see if there was a link between the climate patterns seen in tree rings and the cycle of sunspot activity, which brightens and dims the Sun every 11 years. He found there is a link. Today, dendroclimatologists are able to use the rings in long-lived conifers to create a picture of global and regional climate conditions over the last 7,000 years.

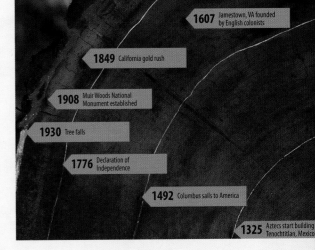

The oldest rings are at the center of the trunk, with the youngest around the edge. Trees have stood witness to many events in human history, and offer a record of climate and atmospheric changes in the distant past.

72 The Richter Scale

EARTHQUAKES ARE THE SINGLE MOST DESTRUCTIVE FORCE ON THE SURFACE OF THE PLANET. Their effects, frequently deadly, can be felt across the globe. In 1935, a system for measuring their power was developed.

VALDIVIA, 1960

Sometimes known as the Great Chilean Earthquake, the quake that hit Valdivia, Chile, on May 22, 1960 was the most powerful ever recorded in human history. It hit 9.6 on the Richter Scale, and went on for approximately 10 minutes. The resulting tsunami not only hit southern Chile, it also raced across the Pacific and impacted Hawaii, Japan, the Philippines, New Zealand, Australia, and the Aleutian Islands. The epicenter was under the Andes Mountains, inland from the old colonial city of Valdivia, which was severely damaged (above).

The Richter Scale, named after Charles Richter, who developed it in 1935, is a measure of the energy released in an earthquake. Anyone caught up in a powerful earthquake will testify that the comparative strength of the shaking is not at the forefront of their minds. They are simply hoping it will reduce, not increase, and do so soon. After the earthquake has passed, the destruction, potentially devastating, remains, and the power that made it has become largely irrelevant to those on the ground. However, seismologists are obviously interested in this kind of information because earthquakes provide their main source of data by generating seismic waves that roll through the planet—and reveal its internal structure. The waves are created when the forces pushing on rocks under the ground have grown sufficient to break the rock. With that tension released, the rock shifts underground.

Billions of tons of solid rock moving all of sudden send out ripples of pressure waves in all directions. When these waves reach the surface, they make it shake—literally rise and fall, or shimmy from side to side. Most buildings are not well suited to these kinds of forces and may crack or collapse.

Earthquakes are more likely to occur along pre-existing cracks in Earth's crust. However, it has so far proven impossible to predict when and where

SHAANXI, 1556

The deadliest earthquake in history occurred in 1556 near Shaanxi in central China. It is estimated to have been around 7.9 on the Richter Scale (there were no direct measurements, obviously). That is a big quake certainly, but still a relatively common occurrence. However, the earthquake, which struck on the night of January 23, is estimated to have killed 830,000 people, making it the worst natural disaster in history. The reason for this shockingly big death toll is that the region is known for extensive deposits of loess, which is a very soft rock. Local people lived in yaodongs, which are caves dug into the cliffs (they are still used today, as shown below). The earthquake made many of these cave homes collapse, and all the sleeping occupants were killed. The local population dropped by 60 percent in a matter of minutes.

they will happen. With every quake, the balance of forces pushing and pulling on the fault system changes. At some time and somewhere, it will give again, and the whole system will shift once more. A reliable way of predicting earthquakes would save lives (plus billions of dollars), so seismologists continue to search for one. The Richter Scale was the first step in this search.

Before Richter, the best that seismologists could do was to compare how far away an earthquake's waves were detected. This became more useful with the invention of reliable seismographs in the 1920s. They showed that the amplitude of a seismic wave increased with the severity of a quake. Richter built on the work of others to develop a way of converting the observed amplitudes into a simple logarithmic scale. He set magnitude 1 as being barely perceptible by a human, and from then on every magnitude related to a quake that was 33 times more powerful than the magnitude before. While the Richter Scale is used in public announcements about quakes, today earth scientists use a similar updated system called the moment magnitude scale.

Magnitude	Frequency
10.0	Never recorded
9.0	1 every 50 years
8.0	1 a year
7.0	10–20 a year
6.0	100–150 a year
5.0	1,000–1,500 a year
4.0	10,000–15,000 a year
3.0	100,000 a year
2.0	1–2 million a year
1.0	Millions per year

An earthquake above magnitude 5 can cause damage to buildings. Above 9, and the quake will create almost total destruction.

73 Earth's Iron Core

IN 1774 THE ASTRONOMER NEVIL MASKELYNE MEASURED THE GRAVITY OF A SCOTTISH MOUNTAIN and used that to calculate the density of Earth. It showed there was something heavy deep inside the planet.

Inge Lehmann received many awards and accolades for her discovery. And she had a long time to enjoy her success by living to the age of 104.

The overall density of the planet is much higher than that of your average rock. The extra weight, it was suggested, came from a heavy core, most probably made from iron and nickel. In 1926, the British geophysicist Harold Jeffreys provided definite proof of this, and from the way seismic waves were blocked by the core, he thought it must be made from a hot, liquid metal. In 1930, the Danish seismologist Inge Lehmann took the opportunity of a sizable earthquake in New Zealand the year before to have a closer look inside Earth. In the seismograms Lehmann saw that certain seismic waves were reflecting off something inside the Earth's liquid core. Jeffreys' liquid core was about 6,800 km (4,250 miles) across. Lehmann suggested that inside that there was an inner core that was about 2,800 km (1,750 miles) across. (She was not far wrong. Today, the inner core is measured at 2442 km [1,526 miles] wide.)

In 1940, it was proposed that Lehmann's inner core is actually a vast ball of solid metal. It is still very hot, hot enough to melt iron, but the great pressure down there keeps it solid. The inner core spins inside the molten outer core. It is presumed that the gooey transition between the solid and liquid portions makes the outer core a complex swirl of currents and eddies. This motion is the best explanation for how Earth's powerful magnetic field—which is second only to Jupiter's in the Solar System—is created.

74 Classifying Minerals

TODAY, MINERALS ARE ORGANIZED ACCORDING TO THE NICKEL–STRUNZ CLASSIFICATION SYSTEM. First proposed in 1941, and regularly updated since, this system is based on chemistry and crystal structure.

The first version of the mineral scheme was simply the Strunz system, named for the German geologist Karl Hugo Strunz. As curator of minerals at Berlin's Humboldt University, he decided to organize the specimens by chemical properties. He opted for dividing minerals into ten classes. In 2001, the American Ernest Nickel revised the classification, and it has been called the Nickel–Strunz system ever since.

CLASSIFICATION OF MINERALS

Gold

1. ELEMENTS
This group includes the elements that occur naturally in their pure, or native, state. Native elements include metals such as gold and silver, plus non-metals including sulfur and carbon (in the form of diamond, graphite, and coal).

Pyrite

2. SULFIDES AND SULFOSALTS
This class is made up of compounds that contain sulfide ions. Generally that ion is bonded to a metal. Several members of this class are important ores. Another member is pyrite, a sulfide mineral better known as fool's gold.

Halite

3. HALIDES
These minerals are compounds of halogens, such as chlorine, fluorine, and iodine. The most significant is halite, which is the mineral form of sodium chloride, better known as common salt.

Sapphire

4. OXIDES AND HYDROXIDES
Most of the minerals in this class are simple oxides, and include ores of copper and iron, plus ice, the solid form of water. In addition, several gems such as ruby and sapphire are in the class.

Calcite

5. CARBONATES AND NITRATES
Made up of compounds with ions composed of carbon and oxygen, or more rarely nitrogen and oxygen, this class includes calcite and the chalk-like minerals in limestones. Saltpeter, a nitrate mineral, is an ingredient in gunpowder.

6. BORATES
This is one of the smaller classes in the system. A borate is a compound that includes boron and oxygen. The most familiar member is borax, which has a history of use in cleaning products.
Borax

7. SULFATES AND ALLIES
In contrast to Class 2, these sulfur-rich compounds also contain oxygen atoms. In addition, the class includes the chromates, molybdates, and tungstates, which are chemically similar although rarer.
Barite

8. PHOSPHATES AND ALLIES
The minerals in this class, which are dominated by phosphorus, but also include arsenates and vanadates, are numerous but hard to find. One of the most common is apatite, a natural form of calcium phosphate, which is the material in tooth enamel.
Muscovite

9. SILICATES
This diverse group, which is based on silicon dioxide units arranged in a number of patterns, makes up 90 percent of Earth's rocks. The group includes the micas and the feldspars.
Datolite

10. ORGANIC COMPOUNDS
Some geologists do not regard these materials as minerals because they are not made by geological processes. Instead, they are ultimately created by biological processes. This class includes amber, which is a fossilized form of tree resin
Amber

75 Weather Radar

RADAR WAS AN INNOVATION OF WORLD WAR II, AND OPERATORS SCANNING THE SKIES FOR ENEMY AIRCRAFT often picked up false signals from approaching rain clouds. In peacetime that offered a new forecasting tool.

Modern weather radar uses the Doppler effect to detect the direction in which the weather system is moving.

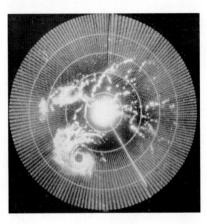

Radar is a system that uses pulses of radio waves to detect objects far beyond the horizon. The radio waves reflect off any objects they hit—be they a fleet of aircraft or clouds producing sheets of rain—and the resulting radio echo received back at the radar station tells operators what is out there. Canadian radar scientists found ways to correlate the intensity of the radar echo with the strength of rain, while a British team linked echo patterns with cloud types. Weather radar was able to watch weather systems develop, including tornado outbreaks. This not only resulted in better radar, but also in a better understanding of meteorology. By the 1980s, weather radar was a normal tool for weather forecasting.

76 Ediacara: A Lost Form of Life

IT USED TO BE THOUGHT THAT LIFE ARRIVED ON EARTH IN THE CAMBRIAN PERIOD, STARTING AROUND 540 MILLION YEARS AGO. Then a find in the Ediacara Hills in South Australia forced people to reconsider.

The Ediacaran Dickinsonia *has been described as a primitive plant, a fungus, or perhaps a segmented animal. Perhaps it represents an entirely different, and now extinct, kingdom of life.*

In 1946, Reg Sprigg, an Australian paleontologist, began to find what he assumed were jellyfish in rocks that he dated as being from the very early days of the Cambrian. Similar fossils had been found elsewhere, with some appearing in even older rocks, but that contravened the firm belief that life began in the Cambrian. So, these strangely shaped structures were explained away as artifacts left by ripples and bubbles in the sediment.

However, by the 1960s, it was clear that Sprigg's fossils represented multicellular life that lived around 575 million years ago, predating the Cambrian. Known as the Ediacaran biota, these strange fossils resembled fern fronds, flatworms, and pillbugs all at the same time. Were they our earliest ancestors? They suddenly disappeared as the Cambrian Explosion started, so perhaps they were an alternative form of life that did not survive.

77 Microfossils

WHILE THE JURY WAS OUT ON THE AGE OF THE EDIACARAN BIOTA, ANOTHER FOSSIL DISCOVERY IN THE GUNFLINT RANGE of Minnesota in 1953 reset the geological and biological timelines in a very big way.

Animals, plants, and fungi are not the only living things on Earth. Since the 18th century it has been known that there is also an invisible world of microscopic organisms, things like bacteria, yeasts, and amoebas. At first, the paleontology of microbes was largely concerned with biological sediments, such those that made certain limestones and chalks. Under a microscope, the calcium-rich fragments appear as the shells, or tests, of microscopic sea creatures, which have sunk to the seabed after the soft parts of the animal decayed away. These deposits were all formed during the Paleozoic and Mesozoic, the time in Earth's history when complex life was already present. (For example, the Cretaceous, from 145 to 66 million years ago, is named after the vast chalk deposits formed by the tests of coccolithophore algae.)

However, Gunflint Range contains a layer of chert that is nearly 1.9 billion years old. It contains layers of red iron and black silica. In 1953, the fossil hunter Stanley Tyler examined the black layer under a microscope and found small spheres and rod-shaped objects around 10 micrometers long. They looked a lot like bacteria cells, and later analysis revealed that they were photosynthetic cyanobacteria. This discovery wound back the start point of life. A new eon of life—the Proterozoic—had been found which covers the time when Earth had only simple, single-celled life. The current understanding is that the first bacteria-like organisms evolved 2.5 billion years ago.

Fossil microorganisms, like the ones in the Gunflint chert, form stromatolites. These striped fossils are made from millions of layers of bacteria, where a new generation grows on the remains of the last.

78 Mid-Atlantic Ridge

THE CHALLENGER EXPEDITION OF THE 1870S FOUND A REGION OF RUGGED SEABED IN THE MIDDLE OF THE ATLANTIC. In 1953, this was revealed as the longest mountain range in the world—hidden beneath the ocean.

The researchers aboard HMS *Challenger* were surveying a possible route for a transatlantic telegraph cable. Later researchers had a more scientific interest in the submarine features. They were aided by the invention of the echo-sounder, which pings high-pitched sound signals into the water and picks up any echoes from the seabed. This was a faster and more accurate method of mapping the depth of water than earlier sounding techniques. By 1925, soundings made by *Meteor*, a German research ship, showed that the rugged seabed appeared to form a long range of submerged peaks that curved around the southern tip of Africa and entered the Indian Ocean.

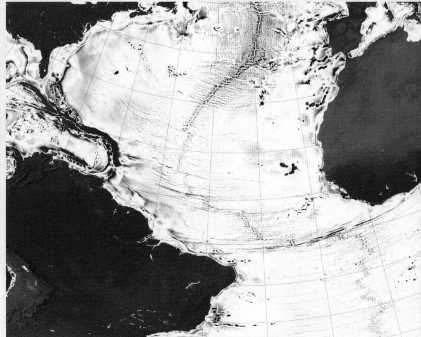

Oceanography was revolutionized by the invention of the fathometer, an echo-sounding system created by Herbert Grove Dorsey in 1928.

Looking deeper

It was not until the 1950s that a clear map of the entire system was created, thanks in the main to the work of American geologists and mapmakers Maurice Ewing, Bruce Heezen, and Marie Tharp. Ewing and Heezen collected sounding data aboard the research ship *Verna*. Barred as a woman from working "in the field" on a research ship, back in New York Tharp combined this information with other data about the ocean floor that had been collected by researchers at the Woods Hole Oceanographic Institution in Massachusetts. In 1953 she revealed the clearest map of the whole Atlantic seabed to date, showing that running down the middle was an other-worldly feature of tall ridges with deep valleys in between. This was the Mid-Atlantic Ridge, which later research revealed is actually just one section of an underwater mountain range that runs from the Arctic to the eastern Indian Ocean. It was soon clear that the ridge was very seismically active (and still is), and volcanic islands, such as Iceland, formed where the ridge broke the surface.

The Mid-Atlantic Ridge zigzags across the ocean floor and never gets close to the continents either side.

79 Climate Modeling

WEATHER FORECASTING TAKES STARTING CONDITIONS AND ATTEMPTS TO USE THEM TO PREDICT how conditions will have changed by a point in the future. Is it possible to model the entire planet?

COMPUTER FORECASTING

The first person to use mathematics to predict the weather was the Briton Lewis Richardson. In 1922 he produced a forecast for six hours into the future based on the state of the atmosphere. However, it took him six weeks to do this by hand—by which time his forecast was very late. To speed things up, some kind of programmable calculating machine was needed. Perhaps we could call it a computer? By the late 1940s, one of the first electronic computers (ENIAC, above) was built for the U.S. Army, and in 1950 it was used to compute a weather forecast. It used a simplistic system, but could produce results fast enough to be a useful predictor. In 1954, Swedish meteorologists used the ENIAC program for regular forecasting.

In 1956, Norman Phillips, a meteorologist working at the Institute for Advanced Study at Princeton, wrote a mathematical system to model the way the troposphere changed month to month. When run on a computer, it created a realistic climate model, able to speed up time and show the state of the atmosphere and oceans many years into the future. It was complete with weather systems and maps of the winds blowing at the surface as well as at the boundary with the stratosphere (the so-called jet stream). Phillips's general circulation model was the first climate model. It was deemed a great success, although no one believed that it gave an accurate prediction of what was going to happen to the climate next year or the year after that. What it did show was that weather and climate are phenomena that could be modeled with mathematics and enough computing power. Since Phillips's breakthrough, climate models have been constantly refined to behave ever more like the true Earth system.

NOAA CLIMATE MODEL

-20 -16 -13 -11 -9 -7 -5 -3.6 -2.8 -2 -1.2 -0.4 0.4 1.2 2 2.8 3.6 5 7 9 11 13 16 20 °F

Surface Air Temperature change [°F]

(2050s average minus 1971-2000 average)

A climate model from the U.S. National Oceanic and Atmospheric Administration shows its predictions of changes in the average temperatures across the globe in 2050.

80 Weather Satellite

IN THE EARLIEST DAYS OF THE SPACE RACE, PEOPLE WERE IMAGINING THE BENEFITS OF A SYSTEM for monitoring weather from space. By the start of the 1960s, satellite data was improving our forecasts.

The first artificial vehicles to make it into space were flying bombs developed by the Germans. Once commandeered by American scientists, some saw the civilian benefits of this technology (although the bomb theme still had plenty of backers). If a satellite could send back live pictures of the atmosphere from space, it would send weather forecasting out of this world. So that is what they did.

Into space

Early systems simply flung cameras to high altitude using rockets in suborbital flights, but the data collected was of little use and did not warrant the expense. By 1959, there were two rival satellite systems in development. The first into orbit was Vanguard, which was developed by the U.S. Army Signal Corps. Its mission was to measure the location and thickness of clouds. However, in the early days of space technology there was much to learn and much to get wrong. Vanguard spun at the wrong angle to get a good view of Earth's surface, and its elliptical orbit, while easier to achieve with the launch vehicles available, was ill-suited to monitoring the surface of Earth. Vanguard was scrapped, and NASA's TIROS program of 1960 proved more successful. By the end of the decade, NASA's Nimbus satellites were collecting temperature as well as cloud data. Today's weather satellites take detailed scans of Earth's surface, with microwave radar being used to detect wind patterns.

TIROS stood for Television Infrared Observation Satellites. The satellites sent back video of Earth's clouds.

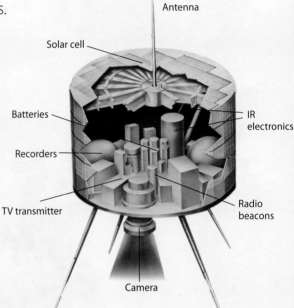

Antenna
Solar cell
Batteries
Recorders
TV transmitter
IR electronics
Radio beacons
Camera

TIROS satellites were only in orbit for about 80 days. Today's versions are put into high geostationary orbits where they can stay for many years.

VAN ALLEN BELTS

The first American spacecraft was Explorer 1, which was launched in a hurry in January 1958, to compete with the Soviets' successful Sputnik 1 and 2 the year before. Explorer 1's launch vehicle could not make orbit, unlike the Sputniks, but despite the barely hidden subtext of Cold War rivalry, the spacecraft was launched under the pretext of a geophysical experiment—and it produced results. Explorer discovered intense bands of magnetism high above Earth. These are named the Van Allen Belts for the NASA scientist who identified them. The Van Allen Belts are responsible for deflecting charged particles in solar wind around Earth. This material is funneled toward the poles, where it creates the aurora phenomena when it hits the atmosphere.

81 Plate Tectonics

THE WORK OF MANY MINDS HAD REVEALED THAT CONTINENTS DRIFTED, THAT EARTHQUAKES CRACKED ROCKS APART, and that the Earth's crust floated on a sea of magma. The theory of plate tectonics put all that together.

Earth's crust is a thin shell of rock around the whole planet. Only it is broken into a dozen plates, which bump and grind together, making and breaking solid rock and changing the geography of Earth.

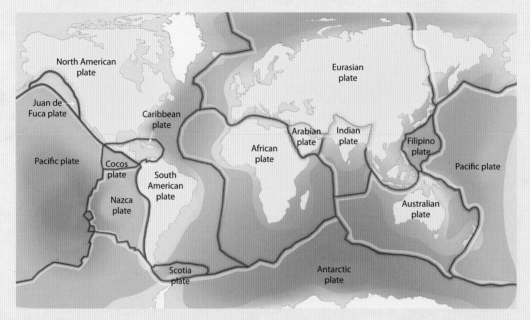

The leading figure in continental drift theory, Alfred Wegener, needed to back up his claim with a mechanism by which landmasses could sail around the world. He proposed that the continents, made mostly from low-density granite, floated on a "sea" of denser basalt, which is the main igneous rock that forms the seabed. The continents, he said, plowed through the seabed, like an iceberg bobbing along in the sea.

Harry Hess runs through the basics of plate tectonics to explain how the surface of Earth is constantly shifting in shape.

More and more evidence suggested that continental drift was correct. Among the most conclusive was paleomagnetism, which showed that iron in rocks was aligned to Earth's magnetic field when the rocks formed, although they had since shifted out of alignment. This proved that rocks and the continents they formed are wandering around. But the question of how was still unanswered.

Sea-floor spreading

The crucial breakthrough in developing the theory of plate tectonics (which means "about building") came in 1960 when Harry Hess, an American geologist with unrivaled access to ocean floor surveys, thanks to a strong link to the U.S. Navy, proposed that new crust was

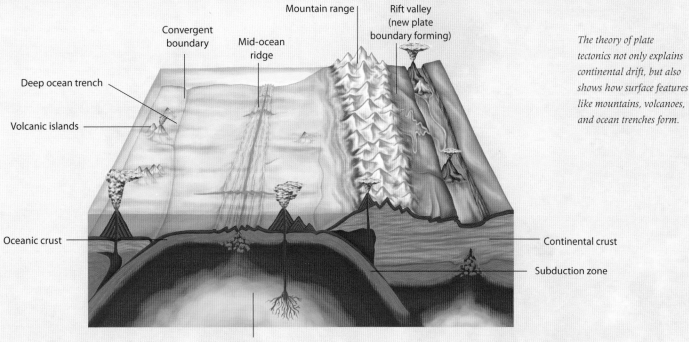

Convergent boundary

Mid-ocean ridge

Mountain range

Rift valley (new plate boundary forming)

Deep ocean trench

Volcanic islands

Oceanic crust

Continental crust

Subduction zone

Magma

The theory of plate tectonics not only explains continental drift, but also shows how surface features like mountains, volcanoes, and ocean trenches form.

being made at the mid-ocean ridges. These are essentially cracks in Earth's crust, where magma wells up to fill the gap and forms new basalt sea-floor. The upwelling magma, driven by convection currents in the mantle—as if the inside of Earth is on a slow boil—continues to drive the cracks apart, and slowly but surely the sea-floor spreads, pushing the ocean's two coasts apart. Transatlantic cables had been known to snap in the past, and this was why. Hess and others later showed that the Atlantic spreads by around 2.5 cm (1 inch) a year.

The crust is divided up into tectonic plates. The mid-ocean ridges form divergent or constructive boundaries, where new crust is made. Other boundaries are convergent, where one plate plunges beneath the other until it melts back into the mantle. These are destructive boundaries, prone to earthquakes, where the plates get rubbed together, or volcanoes, where magma leaks back to the surface. The Pacific Ocean, which is shrinking as the Atlantic spreads, is surrounded by destructive boundaries which connect up to form the Pacific Ring of Fire, the most volcanic region on Earth.

The heat of the interior of Earth drives the process of plate tectonics and continental drift.

82 Marianas Trench

MORE PEOPLE HAVE BEEN INTO SPACE THAN HAVE VISITED CHALLENGER DEEP IN THE MARIANAS TRENCH, the deepest part of the ocean floor. In 1960, the first people to go there used a unique vehicle called a bathyscaphe.

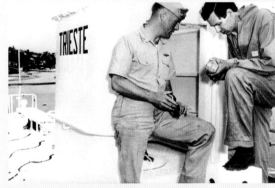

Navy Lieutenant Don Walsh (left) and Swiss scientist Jacques Piccard prepare their vessel before the record-breaking dive.

A bathyscaphe has no form of propulsion, unlike a submarine. It dives by sinking straight down—all the way to the seabed. The bathyscaphe used in the 1960 expedition was called *Trieste*. It was built by the Swiss scientist Auguste Piccard, mostly in Trieste (now in Italy) and was piloted by his son Jacques. The bathyscaphe was owned by the U.S. Navy, and so Lieutenant Don Walsh was also in the crew. The pair sat in a pressure sphere hanging under a vast tank of gasoline. This tank functioned as a float, and the *Trieste* was weighted down with iron pellets, so it sank in water. On January 23, 1960, the *Trieste* sank into the ocean. The descent took five hours, but Walsh and Piccard spent barely 20 minutes on the ocean floor (10,916 m; 35,814 ft down) before releasing the iron pellets and beginning the three-hour journey back. They had planned to stay longer, but the outer window cracked so they prudently opted to return to the surface sooner. The pressure of the water down there is more than 1,000 times as strong as at the surface.

Trieste was 15 m (50 ft) long. The main tank held 85,000 liters (22,000 gallons) of gasoline. There were water ballast tanks at either end to maintain balance. The iron weights were released from cones either side of the crew capsule, which was 2.16 m (7.09 ft) wide.

83 Meteors

AS THE FOUNDER OF ASTROGEOLOGY, EUGENE SHOEMAKER HAS AN ASTEROID, A COMET, AND EVEN A SPACECRAFT named after him. All this work began with a survey of a mysterious crater in the Arizona desert.

Astrogeology compares the rocks of a planet, moon, or other space material with what we know about Earth to unpick their history. Shoemaker was able to draw a conclusive link between all rocks in the Solar System thanks to a discovery in what was then called the Barringer Crater in central Arizona. Earlier explorers had presumed that it was the remains of a volcano, but others suggested it was made by a meteorite—a lump of rock from space. In 1960, Shoemaker found "shocked" silica there, a mineral that he had only seen before at nuclear bomb test sites. It cannot be made by natural volcanic forces; only the energy of a meteorite impact could create it. Shoemaker had provided the first proof that large meteorites with a geology like Earth's rocks hit our planet. What we see down here, we will see out there in space.

The site of Eugene Shoemaker's discovery is now better known as Meteor Crater.

84 Earth's Magnetic Field Flips

THE FIELD OF PALEOMAGNETISM BEGAN IN THE EARLY 1900S WHEN GEOLOGISTS NOTICED THAT SOME ROCKS were magnetized in the opposite way to the direction of Earth's field in that area.

Magnetometers measure the strength and polarity of a magnetic field. Specialized magnetometers were towed over the seabed to detect changes in polarity (or direction) of the magnetic particles frozen inside.

Paleomagnetic research was mostly focused on plotting the motion of continents through geological time to help understand how they moved. By the 1960s, enough evidence had accrued to suggest another phenomenon, that Earth's magnetic field had reversed many times in the remote past. That meant if compasses had existed at the time, during some periods of the past they would have pointed south. Magnetized volcanic rocks preserve traces of the Earth's magnetic field at the time the rocks had cooled. During the investigations into sea-floor spreading, as part of the formulation of the theory of plate tectonics, it became clear that the planet's magnetic field has flipped 181 times in the last 83 million years—and could do so again soon.

85 The Hotspot

IN 1963, A NEW THEORY EMERGED ABOUT HOW ISLAND CHAINS LIKE HAWAII form. This would be the ultimate illustration of sea-floor spreading.

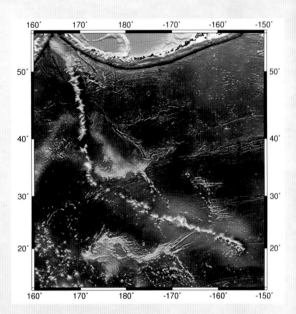

Anyone who has visited Hawaii's "Big Island" will know that the land is of volcanic origin. In most volcanic regions, the volcanoes appear in chains forming along a plate boundary of some kind. However, this is not the case in Hawaii. Most of the other islands in the state do not have active volcanoes. J. Tuzo Wilson developed the idea of a hotspot to explain this. He proposed that the Hawaiian Islands formed one by one as the Pacific plate moved over a plume of hot magma surging up through the crust—a hotspot. This hotspot fed the volcanoes at the surface, making an island. Sea-floor spreading steadily moved this island away from the hotspot, but the magma plume was in the mantle, and so stayed where it was. In turn, new islands formed above it and were moved away, with only the newest island still connected to the magma. Quite how the magma gathers in one part of the mantle to create a plume is still an open question.

Seen from space, the Hawaiian Islands trace a path across the ocean.

86 The Formation of Earth

WHAT CAN THE EARTH SCIENCES TELL US about the formation of the planet? A theory from 1969 remains the best explanation.

The idea that Earth and the other planets in the Solar System somehow coalesced from a nebula—a fuzzy blob of materials such as dust and gas—is an old one. However, it was given a clear process by the Russian astronomer Viktor Safronov in 1969 with the publication of his solar nebula theory.

This theory says that, first, the Sun formed from a contracting ball of gas. In the process, the remaining

The planets formed from a disc-shaped solar nebula.

material formed into a spinning disc. The heavier constituents, grains of silicate and metal, orbited nearer the young star, while lightweight ices were further out, where it was cold enough for them to stay frozen. Little by little, these materials bumped together and began to clump into bigger and bigger objects, called planetesimals. The pull of gravity took over, and these planetesimals swept up more material as they grew into planets.

Earth formed from the heavy minerals and metals that gathered near the Sun. For millions of years meteor impacts were more or less constant, heating the planet into a ball that was almost entirely molten. At this stage, the denser metal components sunk to the middle of the young planet, forming the metallic core, while the lighter silicates created the mantle, and eventually cooled enough to form a solid crust.

The Kepler space telescope, in action from 2009 to 2018, scanned the sky for planets that orbit other stars. What will we learn from those distant planets?

87 NOAA

STANDING FOR NATIONAL OCEANIC AND ATMOSPHERIC ADMINISTRATION, THE UNITED STATES' leading earth sciences organization was established in 1970, but has a much longer and venerable history.

NOAA, pronounced "noah" like the Biblical shipbuilder, can trace its history all the way back to 1807 when Congress demanded a thorough survey of the coast of the new country. The United States Survey of the Coast was the first government science agency in American history. By 1917, the organization had been renamed the U.S. Coast and Geodetic Survey, and its personnel were made commissioned officers in a uniformed service alongside the army, navy, and others. The reason was to afford protection to surveyors who might be captured by an enemy power. Their uniform clearly identified them so they could not be treated as spies. During the 20th century, other earth science agencies and services were steadily added. For example the U.S, Weather Bureau was absorbed in 1965. Then in 1970, President Richard Nixon converted the patchwork of earth science agencies into NOAA, with the view that it would offer "better protection of life and property from natural hazards …for a better understanding of the total environment … [and] the intelligent use of our marine resources." As well as carrying out research into the oceans and Earth's atmosphere, the new agency was also given the job of looking after fisheries and marine reserves, dealing with droughts, and managing a fleet of satellites.

A NOAA team chases a storm to find out more about how tornadoes work.

88 Superdeep Boreholes

PLATE TECTONICS AND MANY OTHER THEORIES OF PHYSICAL GEOLOGY RELY ON THE MANTLE BEING A PLIABLE OATMEAL OF HOT ROCK. But that is just a clever guess. No one has ever collected a sample of material from the mantle. Time to go deep—really deep.

The Kola Superdeep Borehole drilling rig before the site was sealed in 1995.

In 1961, the exploration of Earth's interior was being treated as a twin project (the quieter twin) of the Space Race. The United States launched Project Mohole, cleverly named to explain it was a plan to drill a hole to the Moho (see more, page 81). Beneath continental landmasses, the Moho can be 65 km (40 miles) down, but in certain parts of the seabed, the oceanic crust is only 6 km (3.7 miles) thick, perhaps even less. However, drilling through miles of rock from ships floating high above the seabed proved harder than going into space. Project Mohole, drilling in 3,600 m (11,700 ft) of water, managed to collect samples from 183 m (601 ft) in the rocky crust. That was deeper than ever before and so of great geological interest, but it was still a long way short of the Moho.

Kola borehole

In 1970, the Soviet Union tried to beat the United States to the mantle. They took a different approach by choosing to drill on land, creating the Kola Superdeep Borehole in northwestern Russia. This drilling operation continued until 1992, and the project was officially shutdown in 1995. So how did it do in all that time? Several boreholes were drilled from a central entry point, each one just 23 cm (9 inches) wide. By 1989 the deepest borehole had reached 12,262 meters (7.619 miles). The team pressed on with the aim of reaching the target depth of 15,000 m (49,000 ft) by 1993. However, the temperature of the rock at the 1989 depth was 180°C (356°F), and that extra heat made it impossible for drilling equipment to go any deeper. The Kola borehole remains the deepest hole on Earth, although it is still a long way from the Moho. (Oilfields have longer holes but they do not go straight down. The current record is a 12,345-m [40,502 ft] hole off the Siberian coast.)

The latest plan to reach the mantle is the international Project SloMo, which is drilling into a sea-floor ridge in the Indian Ocean where the mantle is only 2.5 km (1.5 miles) down. So far the drill is about half way there.

89 Tornadoes

WHIRLWINDS AND TWISTERS ARE NOT UNHEARD OF OUTSIDE THE UNITED STATES, but nowhere else suffers so frequently from their destructive power. In 1971, a tornado grading system was introduced to help people prepare for the potential danger.

A tornado is a funnel of rotating air that connects the base of a cumulonimbus cloud to the ground. The air pressure inside the funnel is very low, perhaps 80 percent of a regular sea-level reading. Updrafts suck material into the cloud, and the pressure change can, in extreme cases, make buildings literally explode. The average tornado has a wind speed of 180 km/h (110 mph) or less, is 80 m (250 ft) wide, and only lasts for a few minutes before disappearing. However, at the extreme end, a tornado could be 3 km (2 miles) across and have winds whirling around at 480 km/h (300 mph), leaving a path of destruction 100 km (60 miles) long.

The ability to predict tornadoes began in 1948 when two of them hit Tinker Air Force Base in Oklahoma within days of each other. The base's weather station showed their common starting conditions. In 1971, Tetsuya "Ted" Fujita introduced a scale that ran from F0, the weakest grade, to F5, the most damaging. While based on wind speed within the twister, the Fujita scale is really an assessment of damage, and is retrospectively applied so emergency services are directed to where they are most needed.

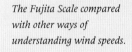

The Fujita Scale compared with other ways of understanding wind speeds.

SUPER OUTBREAK

The 1974 Super Outbreak was the most violent tornado outbreak in history. In 24 hours on April 3 and 4, 148 tornadoes formed across 13 U.S. States—in the so-called Tornado Alley that runs from Texas to Michigan—and 30 of them were F4 or above. They caused damage worth US$4.5 billion in today's prices and killed 335 people. A super outbreak in 2011 had more tornadoes—216—but they were less powerful. Nevertheless, they hit more urban areas, and caused a death toll of 348 people.

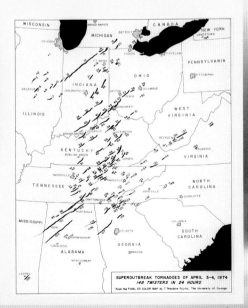

SUPEROUTBREAK TORNADOES OF APRIL 3-4, 1974
148 TWISTERS IN 24 HOURS
From the FINAL ED COLOR MAP by T. Theodore Fujita, The University of Chicago

90 Hydrothermal Vents

IN 1976, DEEP OCEAN EXPLORERS FOUND A HOT SPRING ON THE SEABED, and a weird way of life.

Surveys of deep water occasionally reported finding hot, hypersaline (very salty) water at the bottom of the cold ocean. It was assumed that these waters seeped out somewhere from volcanically active regions of the seabed. Mining prospectors wondered if the rocks in these locations might be filled with valuable metals, but finding the sources of the hot water was difficult in the dark, deep sea. Then, in June 1976, explorers from the Scripps Institution of Oceanography in San Diego found one in the Eastern Pacific near the Galápagos Islands.

Early indications from remotely operated cameras were that the spring—more properly named a hydrothermal vent—was too hot for living things. Water around it was about 60° C (140° F), in contrast to the 2° C (36° F) of the rest of the deep ocean. The Scripps team nicknamed the vent "Clam Bake" (any marine animals close by would be literally cooked by the volcanic water), and made plans to take a closer look in person using the submersible *Alvin* (which was operated by the Woods Hole Oceanographic Institution located over on the East Coast). On arrival at the vent, it soon became apparent that—against all indications to the contrary—it supported a fertile ecosystem, the likes of which had never been seen before.

Some hydrothermal vents can be as high as 464°C (867°F). They are kept liquid by the combination of the great pressures on the seabed and the many dissolved minerals. Often these minerals precipitate into a dark cloud on contact with the cold ocean, creating what is called a "black smoker."

Alvin and other deep-sea submersibles were designed as replacements for the bathyscaphes of the 1960s. They were more maneuverable and were equipped with lights, cameras, and sampling devices.

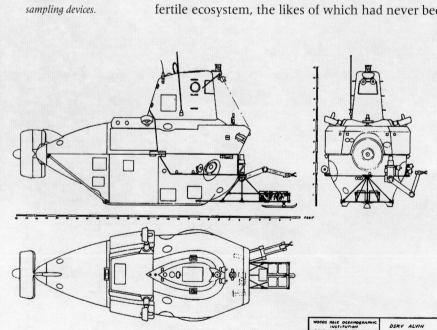

WOODS HOLE OCEANOGRAPHIC INSTITUTION
DEPT. OF OCEAN ENGINEERING
PROJ. 40/2   BY: R. BLAND
SCALE: 3/8"= 1' DATE: 11-13-73

DSRV ALVIN
OUTLINE
DRAWINGS

Chemical eaters

The water that emerges from these vents has percolated through rocks heated by volcanic activity deeper down. When it reaches the seabed, it is rich in minerals, which are used as food by bacteria living in the warm water. Many animals, such as worms and shellfish, allow these bacteria to live inside their bodies in return for a supply of nutrients. This is the only type of ecosystem on Earth that does not rely on a source of solar energy.

91 Mass Extinctions

AROUND 66 MILLION YEARS AGO, THE DINOSAURS AND OTHER GIANT REPTILES THAT ONCE RULED EARTH SUDDENLY BECAME EXTINCT. The event is marked as the end of the Mesozoic era and the start of the Cenozoic. In 1980, a father-and-son team found a clue in rock to the dinosaurs' demise.

Luis (left) and Walter Alvarez at the K-Pg boundary in Italy.

All boundaries in the geologic time scale relate to a global change in the fossil and rock record. The end of the Mesozoic era, which is known as the K–Pg boundary because the Cretaceous period (K) transitioned to the Paleogene (Pg) at the same time, was a big change. It not only saw the loss of large reptiles, but also of all the ammonites and many flowering plants. Why all this life should suddenly disappear was much debated. An old idea was that the dinosaurs got so large and slow that they could not cope with a shift in the climate. Then, in 1980, Luis and Walter Alverez, a veteran nuclear physicist and his geologist son, promoted a much better theory: a big meteorite had hit the Earth at the same time as the extinction. It would have scorched vast swathes of land and sent clouds of dust into the atmosphere that shrouded the entire planet from the Sun for many years. These were the kinds of conditions that led to three-quarters of life on Earth dying out. The Alverezes's proof was the presence of "shocked" quartz, a mineral that can only be formed in a very violent impact. A thin layer of this mineral covered the whole planet at the K-Pg boundary. The Alverez Hypothesis did not say where the impact had happened, but in 1990 it was found to be Chicxulub in southern Mexico, where a 150-kilometer (93 mile) crater is now mostly submerged by the Caribbean Sea. It is estimated that it was formed by a space rock up to 80 km (50 miles) wide!

There have been five mass extinctions, with the most recent one, the Cretaceous–Paleogene event, being relatively mild.

444 million years ago — Present day

Ordovician–Silurian | Late Devonian | Permian–Triassic | Triassic–Jurassic | Cretaceous–Paleogene

Extinct animals (left to right): Graptolites Trilobites Tabulate corals Crinoids Ammonites				
Extinction Event	Ordovician–Silurian	Late Devonian	Permian–Triassic (*Great Dying*)	Triassic–Jurassic	Cretaceous–Paleogene
Date	444 million years ago	375 million years ago	251 million years ago	200 million years ago	66 million years ago
Impact	86% of species lost	75% of species lost	96% of species lost	80% of species lost	76% of species lost

92 Lahar

VOLCANIC ERUPTIONS HAVE ALL TOO OFTEN BEEN SUDDEN AND DEADLY TRAGEDIES. IN 1985, THE WORLD bore witness to a lesser-known volcanic threat that destroyed the town of Armero.

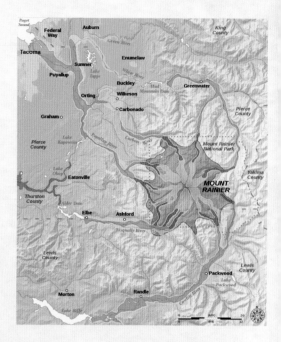

On the night of November 13, 1985, the Nevado del Ruiz volcano in Tolima, Colombia, erupted. It was not unexpected, since volcanologists had warned about increased activity over the previous two months. However, the local community was not too worried. Historically, eruptions did not encroach onto inhabited areas. But during this eruption, a pyroclastic flow, a fast current of gas and, in this case, superheated ash, melted the glaciers on the mountain. This began a series of torrents and mudslides called a lahar. In total, four lahars moved down the mountain at speeds of 50 km/h (30 mph). They picked up more speed as they were funneled into gullies and flowed out into the six major rivers that were fed by the mountain's watershed. Two of the lahars combined at a river tributary about 20 km (12.5 miles) from the eruptions, and 15 km (9 miles) further down slope, this mass of mud, water, and rocks engulfed the town of Armero. Most of the 29,000 inhabitants were asleep, and more than 20,000 of them died as the lahar buried their homes. Another 3,000 people were killed as lahars hit other towns. This was the second-deadliest volcanic disaster of the 20th century, and largely avoidable if evacuation procedures had been followed.

This map from the USGS shows the danger zones around Mount Rainier, a tall volcano in Washington State. The areas marked in green, orange, and red are at risk of lahars.

A lahar has left a scar on the landscape after cutting through a mountain community in Indonesia.

93 Ozone Hole

IN THE LATE 1920S, AN ARTIFICIAL TYPE OF GAS WAS INVENTED AS A SAFE REPLACEMENT FOR MORE TOXIC REFRIGERANTS AND PROPELLANTS. Known as chlorofluorocarbons or CFCs, these gases turned out to pose a global threat.

The Dupont lab that produced a commercial form of CFC gas was looking for a chemically inert substance. Scientists assumed that the great strength of the bond between the chlorine, fluorine, and carbon atoms would never be broken in natural conditions, and so the gas would pose no threat. Testing showed as much, and the new gases replaced toxic and explosive chemicals in aerosol cans and refrigerators. When no longer needed, the gas was simply released into the air and forgotten about.

In 1973, two chemists, American F. Sherwood Rowland and Mexican Mario Molina, from the University of California, took a closer look at what CFCs might be doing in the atmosphere. They discovered that CFCs reached the middle of the stratosphere before being broken up by ultraviolet radiation. The pair then realized that this decay process would release free chlorine atoms, which would react with the ozone in the stratosphere. (Ozone is a rare form of oxygen where three atoms are bonded into a molecule, instead of the normal two.) Ozone is toxic to animals, but in the stratosphere the ozone layer provides a shield against high-energy ultraviolet light. In 1985, the British Antarctic Survey reported that Molina and Rowland's fears were justified. CFCs had created a vast hole over the Antarctic. If CFCs were allowed to build up further, the whole of Earth's ozone might disappear, with untold consequences to life unused to exposure to harmful UV rays. In a rare example of international unity, within 18 months a worldwide ban on CFCs (The Montreal Protocol) had been agreed.

Mario Molina (above) and Sherwood Roland shared the 1995 Nobel Prize in Chemistry with Paul J. Crutzen, a Dutch atmospheric scientist and expert in the ozone layer.

An illustration of the growth, and now shrinkage, of the ozone hole over the last few decades. Blue colors reveal where the ozone in the high atmosphere is depleted.

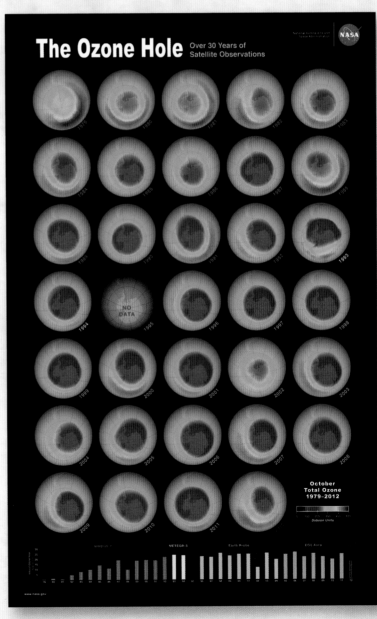

94 Snowball Earth

THE IDEA OF ICE AGES BECAME AN ACCEPTED FACT MORE THAN A CENTURY AGO. IN 1992 A MORE RADICAL IDEA WAS PROPOSED. Had the planet chilled out so much in the distant past that it had frozen over completely? And was this sudden freeze perhaps linked to the rise of life as we know it?

The headline phrase for this idea is the Snowball Earth hypothesis, which was coined by the American geologist Joseph Kirschvink in 1992. However, the idea of a global glaciation event at some point in the past—perhaps even several—had been knocking around in geophysical circles for a long time. One of the theories came from Douglas Mawson, an Australian geologist who found evidence of glaciation in the Precambrian rocks of his home country. This suggested to Mawson that the whole world—at least the land—had once been covered in glaciers. How else could a subtropical place like Australia have been frozen? Mawson was working in the early 1950s, before evidence for continental drift had outweighed the opinions stacked against it. So the idea that Australia was once at much colder latitudes did not figure in his assessments. Nevertheless, the idea of a frozen Earth was never quite dismissed.

Magnetic messages

In the 1960s, as part of the research into continental drift and plate tectonics, paleomagnetic data showed that when glacial deposits were laid down in what is now Svalbard and Greenland, these landmasses were much further to the south, in tropical latitudes. Further work suggested that the glaciation at this time was so extreme that the ocean was freezing solid even in the tropics.

How and when?

There are several mechanisms which could cause this. One could be the effect of albedo, when an icier, whiter planet reflected away more heat (see box, left). Or there might have been a sudden reduction in carbon dioxide, which would lessen the planet's greenhouse effect so it would shed more heat than previously. Climate modeling confirmed that a much colder climate, where Earth's surface was largely frozen, could use these effects to stay cold for a long period.

ALBEDO

Dark surfaces absorb light and heat, while pale ones reflect these energies. Therefore the albedo, or reflectiveness of Earth, increases as the amount of ice on its surface increases. In the 1960s, a Russian climatologist, Mikhail Budyko, suggested this process could create a feedback loop, where a cooling climate was driven to ever colder temperatures because heat from the Sun was being reflected away. Was this a mechanism that created a Snowball Earth?

OXYGEN CATASTROPHE

Air is 21 percent oxygen today, but it was not always so. Oxygen is only in the air because lifeforms keep pumping it out by the process of photosynthesis. Prior to life doing this, Earth's atmosphere had much more carbon dioxide in it. The earliest lifeforms did not use oxygen, and when photosynthesis began to release the gas, it would have proved toxic to most of life on Earth, creating a mass extinction called the Oxygen Catastrophe. Banded ironstones (left) form when oxygen reacts with pure iron to make layers of red hematite. It is a sure sign of a time when there was a surge of oxygen in the air.

According to Joseph Kirschvink, the Snowball Earth was likely to have been in the Proterozoic eon, before the emergence of complex life. He suggested it lasted for 100 million years, and the sea would have been almost completely frozen apart from some open water near the Equator. Others have suggested that the glaciation was not that extreme and would be better characterized as a Slushball Earth, with several areas regularly thawing and refreezing. Snow or slush, this chilly part of Earth's history is now called the Cryogenian period. Another candidate for a Snowball Earth is the Huronian Glaciation, the oldest and longest glaciation in Earth's history, which ran from 2.4 to 2.1 billion years ago. It occurred just after the evolution of photosynthesis had caused the Oxygen Catastrophe (see box, above). This saw oxygen levels rise rapidly, with a corresponding collapse in carbon dioxide levels creating a much cooler climate.

95 The Argo Project

IN 1999, A GROUP OF OCEANOGRAPHERS MET IN MARYLAND TO PLAN AN INTEGRATED OBSERVATION STRATEGY. THEIR GOAL WAS TO update the way data was collected from the oceans. The result was Argo.

In the early 1990s, the Jason satellite was launched to monitor the shape of ocean surfaces (they have bulges and dips caused by tides, winds, and currents). Jason was named after the legendary Greek sailor. So when oceanographers decided to set up a sea-based survey system to compliment the data collected by the satellite, they decided to call the project Argo, after Jason's boat (his crew were the Argonauts). In just eight years, Argo was able to launch 3,000 floating probes for creating real-time maps of the way ocean temperature and salinity change.

Each Argo float sends back data by satellite link. It is also designed to sink below the surface at programed intervals to collect data from different depths. It does this by pumping oil into and out of a rubber bladder to change its density. So far, Argo floats have sent back more than a million readings.

Each Argo float lasts about four years. There are currently around 300 floats working at any one time.

96 Making the Moon

THE MOON IS AROUND A QUARTER OF THE SIZE OF EARTH. That means that for a planet of such meager size, Earth has a very large moon indeed. Where did we get it from?

THE NEAR SIDE

The Moon always shows the same face to us. However, it does rotate, but its rotation has become locked with Earth's. The time it takes for the Moon to move around Earth is equal to the time it takes for the Moon to rotate on its axis once—and so although both bodies are in a constant spin, the same side of the Moon is always locked toward us. This is the result of Earth's gravity having dragged on the Moon, slowing its rotation until it became in sync, as it is today.

For much of the 20th century the best theory we had on the origin of the Moon was Darwin's. Not Charles Darwin, but that of his son George, an astronomer and geologist. At the turn of the century Darwin had proposed that the early Earth, still very hot and therefore soft, was spinning so fast that it flung out a lump or lumps of molten rock and metal. These entered orbit and gradually cooled and coalesced into the Moon.

Moon rock

This so-called fission theory was at first little more than an illustration of the Darwin imagination, being based on no real evidence. However, that changed when the Apollo astronauts returned with their impressive haul of Moon rocks in the 1960s and 1970s. The mineral content of the Moon appeared to be a close match to that of Earth's mantle. That would make sense if it was formed from a blob of the same stuff. The fission theory became a clear front runner, ahead of two rival proposals. The first was accretion theory, which said that Earth and the Moon formed as separate bodies from the same original source material. However, there were problems with this idea. If both bodies formed from the same process, why is the Moon not a small version of Earth? Earth has a large metallic core, which makes the planet almost twice as dense as the Moon, which is thought to have only a small, cold core. Perhaps the Moon was just made somewhere else in the Solar System? This is what the capture theory proposed. The Moon happened to be passing one day and fell into the gravitational control of Earth. However, there are inconsistencies here as well. Other planets have captured moons that have become caught in the drag of their wispy upper atmospheres, which slow down the space rocks enough to trap them in an orbit. But, to capture something as big as the Moon, the early Earth would have had to be surrounded by a preposterously vast, soupy atmosphere.

Two planets hitting each other would have been quite a sight.

A Big Splash

Overall, however, geologists were unconvinced by the fission theory, and after many years of development, an alternative theory took shape by 2000. It even had an impressive name: the giant-impact hypothesis (also known as the Big Splash). After being modeled over and over in computers, the current theory goes like this: Earth was originally 90 percent of its current size. Around 4.4 billion years ago, after Earth had had a few million years to get itself in order, along came another planet, about the size of Mars. This hypothetical planet is called Theia, after the Greek goddess who begat the Sun and the Moon. Theia hit the Earth with a glancing blow that was not enough to shatter both planets, but was enough to melt their surfaces into an ocean of magma, allowing them to merge. The impact also gouged out a chunk of molten material from Earth's mantle, and this formed into an orbital ring system, which eventually accreted into the Moon. This would explain why the minerals in the Moon's rocks are so similar to the ones found in Earth's mantle, and why the Moon's metallic core is so puny compared to that of Earth's (most of Earth's metal was deeper down in the core). As for Earth, the giant-impact hypothesis explains why it has a bigger than average metallic core for its size—after all, a sixth of its other mass is now the Moon. In addition, the impact with Theia ensured that Earth's crust is very thin and prone to cracking, an essential feature of Earth's ever-changing tectonic surface—something not seen on other planets.

The giant-impact hypothesis began with the discovery that Moon rock is filled with the same silicate minerals found deep inside Earth's mantle.

LUNAR SEAS

The most obvious features on the lunar surface are dark regions. Early observers thought these were bodies of water, so named them maria (singular, mare), the Latin for "seas." The lunar maria were then given names, such as Sea of Tranquility. The maria are flat plains formed by volcanic eruptions that flooded lowland regions. Despite dominating our view of the near side of the Moon (pictured, top), maria only cover about 16 percent of its surface. The far side (bottom) is instead covered in rugged highlands. One explanation is that as the Moon was forming from fragments after the Big Splash, two large but unequal objects joined together, giving one side of the Moon a thicker crust than the other. The volcanic eruptions that formed the maria were seldom powerful enough to rupture this thicker side. Instead they only burst out from the thin side.

97 Tsunami

THE TERM *TSUNAMI* MEANS "HARBOR WAVE" IN JAPANESE, A HINT OF THE INSIDIOUS NATURE OF THIS PHENOMENON. In 2004, the world was reminded just how deadly it could be.

A little after dawn on December 26, 2004, an earthquake measuring 9.1 on the Richter Scale hit an epicenter off the west coast of northern Sumatra (a major island in Indonesia) where the Australian Plate meets the Indian Plate. This event was the third largest earthquake ever recorded, and over the course of about 9 minutes, 1,400 km (900 miles) of a fault running through the sea floor shifted, with the lower-density continental rocks of the Australian Plate shifting up by 40 m (130 ft) as the denser Indian Plate sunk beneath it. The energy released was the equivalent of 23,000 atomic bombs of the size dropped on Hiroshima. The motion made the entire planet wobble a centimeter (0.4 inches) off its axis.

Waves hit

Fifteen minutes later, the tsunami warning system set up to detect threats to Hawaii picked up a tremor. However, there was nothing to be done. Five minutes after that, the Sumatran city of Banda Aceh was hit by a 30-meter (100-ft) wave that swamped most of the buildings and killed more than 170,000 people. However, the tsunami wave had spread out in all directions, and about an hour later it hit the coast of Thailand, killing many people on winter beach vacations. As with Banda Aceh, the wave devastated the infrastructure, making it difficult for rescuers to reach the coast and also for the message to spread to other places at risk from the tsunami.

Two hours after the earthquake, the coast of Sri Lanka was hit. The tsunami curved around the island nation's southern coast, killing 30,000 people living in that area. Around the same time, eastern India and Burma were hit, and the wave continued on across the Indian Ocean, spreading out and weakening as it went. However, eight hours after the earthquake, 10-meter (33-ft) waves hit Kenya and Somalia, killing 300

An artist's impression of a tsunami approaching land.

EARLY WARNING SYSTEM

Following the Indian Ocean tsunami, an international warning system was put in place to match the one already in the Pacific Ocean. Seismometers were placed on the seabed to listen out for tremors far from land. These are relayed to a control center, and if necessary, orders to evacuate are now given.

people. Over the course of the day, the Indian Ocean tsunami of 2004 (the event is more officially recorded as the Sumatra–Andaman earthquake) killed 227,989 people in 14 countries.

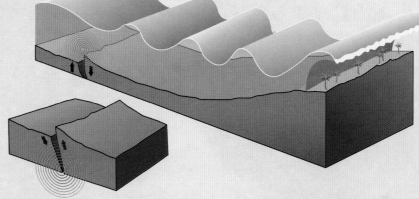

A quiet killer

Without a widespread warning system (see box, left), tsunamis are very hard to defend against. Often mistakenly called tidal waves, they have nothing to do with the ebb and flow of the tides. Instead they are better understood as seismic sea waves which are caused by the displacement of a large volume of water. As well as earthquakes and volcanic eruptions, they can also be caused by submarine rock-slides, icebergs calving off glaciers, and meteorite impacts. The tallest tsunami ever recorded was 524 meters (1720 ft) tall. This monster wave was caused by a rockfall into Lituya Bay, a steep-sided ocean inlet in Alaska.

A shift in the seabed forces the water column to move, and that creates a wave moving at the surface. As the wave enters shallower water, it slows and increases in height until it crashes into land.

Compared to regular ocean waves, tsunami waves have enormously long wavelengths. The distance from one peak to the next can be as much as 500 km (300 miles), and, as a result, the wave height is barely noticeable above mean sea level. Out at sea a tsunami can move at 800 km/h (500 mph), and only when it reaches shallower water, and begins to drag on the seabed, will the wave begin to slow down and rise above the surrounding sea level. This is the root of the idea of "harbor wave." Out at sea, sailors are unaware of the wave, but near the shore it will suddenly rise up.

Tsunamis generally consist of a series of waves (an internal wave train) which arrive minutes or perhaps hours apart. Tsunamis contain so much water that it is common for them to pull water away from the shore at first, as if the tide were going out. When the tsunami arrives a few minutes later it may appear not as a breaking wave, but instead like a rapidly surging tide that rises up along the coast—hence the term "tidal wave." However, the tsunami will flow inland far beyond the normal high water marks.

TSUNAMIS IN WORLD CULTURE

Tsunamis hold an important place in many cultures. Japan, which invented the word and has suffered more earthquakes and tsunamis than any other nation, has a genre of story which often involves a dangerous monster, kaiju, emerging from the ocean and destroying entire cities. In his 1759 story *Candide*, the French writer Voltaire puts his characters in Lisbon during the tsunami of 1755, as a satire of the philosophy of optimism that was being widely discussed at the time.

98 Source of Earth's Water

EARTH IS THE ONLY KNOWN PLANET WHERE THERE IS LIQUID WATER ON THE SURFACE. Why is there so much water here, and where did it all come from? In 2014, a spacecraft flew into deep space to investigate one possibility.

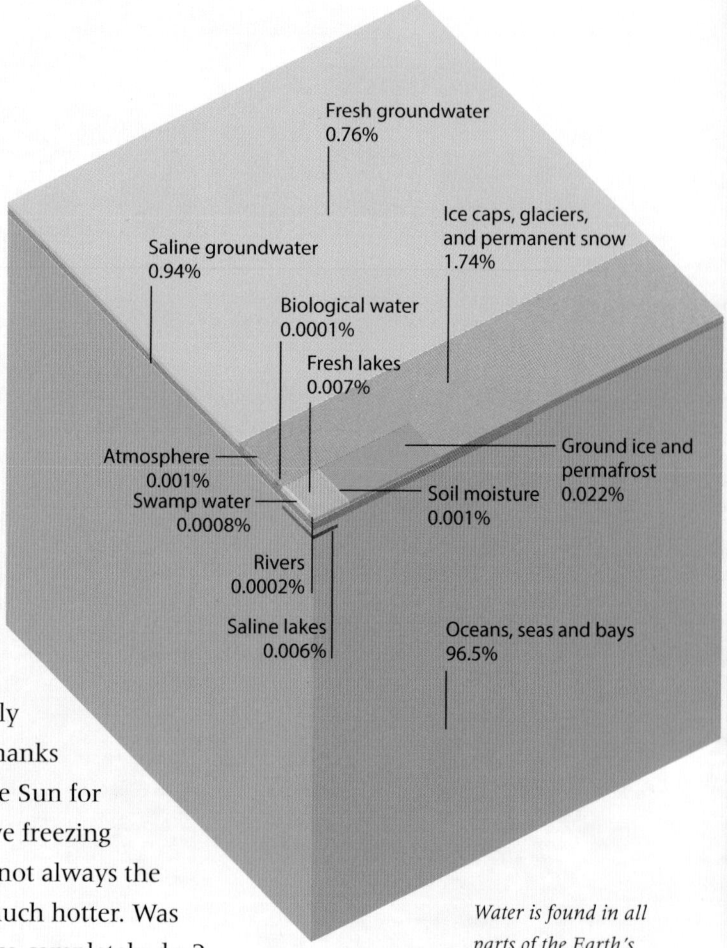

Water is not a rare material in the Solar System. However, most of it is frozen as ice. We know of very few places where liquid water has not frozen due to cold conditions or evaporated away due to low gas pressure. And only one place has liquid on its surface: Earth. This is thanks to the planet orbiting at the right distance from the Sun for the temperature at the surface to mostly stay above freezing point and below boiling point. However, this was not always the case. When Earth was young it must have been much hotter. Was there always an ocean on the surface or was it once completely dry?

Fresh groundwater 0.76%

Ice caps, glaciers, and permanent snow 1.74%

Saline groundwater 0.94%

Biological water 0.0001%

Fresh lakes 0.007%

Atmosphere 0.001%

Swamp water 0.0008%

Ground ice and permafrost 0.022%

Soil moisture 0.001%

Rivers 0.0002%

Saline lakes 0.006%

Oceans, seas and bays 96.5%

Water is found in all parts of the Earth's system. Most of the water vapor is in the lower layer of the atmosphere. Not shown here is water in Earth's mantle, which could contain more water than is found at the planet's surface.

Inside out

When Earth first formed, water, mostly probably as ice, must have been part of the mix of materials, along with frozen carbon dioxide, methane, and some gases like hydrogen and helium. Heavy bombardments by meteorites, not least the Big Splash impact that is conjectured to have formed the Moon (see page 110), probably vaporized the rocks. So Earth's early atmosphere was made of rock vapors! These would have turned back into solid rock within a few centuries. However, that created an atmosphere made up of left-over materials, such as water vapor and carbon dioxide. The levels of carbon dioxide probably went up and down many times over, but water vapor was consistently "out-gassed" from the interior of the planet. This resulted in more and more water gathering in the atmosphere. There are zircon crystals that are more than 4.4 billion

UNDERGROUND OCEAN

Ringwoodite is a form of magnesium silicate that forms at high pressures and temperatures, as found in Earth's mantle around 600 km (375 miles) under the surface. Ringwoodite crystals from the mantle show evidence of forming in water. This suggests that the upper mantle could be very wet and contain three times as much water as is at the surface.

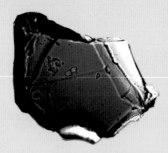

years old, so at least part of Earth's surface was solid at that time, and has remained so ever since. Crucially, however, zircons need liquid water to form. Under the heavy carbon dioxide atmosphere of the early Earth, water would have stayed liquid up to a temperature of 230 °C (446 °F)! In these conditions, atmospheric water vapor would have formed the first clouds and fallen as the first rains in the very early days of Earth's history. The water gathered in what would become the oceanic basins, and has been doing so ever since. However, did Earth's interior contain all the water we now see on the surface. Or did a lot of it come from outer space?

The tail of a comet, like 67P, above, forms when the ice interior is heated by the Sun and begins to stream away as a dusty streak of water vapor.

Outside in?

The word comet comes from the Greek for "hairy star" in allusion to the streaky tail that forms around these occasional visitors. However, a better name is "dirty snowball," because comets are made from water ice mixed with dust and sooty substances. Comets come from the distant edge of the Solar System and represent material left over from the formation of the planets. Perhaps Earth's huge supply of water came from millions of comets that smashed into Earth in the first few hundred million years of its existence. In 2004, a European spacecraft called Rosetta was launched to take a look. Ten years later it met up with Comet 67P/Churyumov–Gerasimenko, but better known as just 67P, far beyond the orbit of Mars. A lander was sent to touch down on the surface and worked with the orbiter to analyse the chemical signatures in the water (among many other things). The water, on 67P at least, did not match Earth's. Perhaps our oceans did not arrive from space after all.

THE LARGEST OCEAN KNOWN

Earth's global ocean is impressive, but it is not even the largest in the Solar System. Europa is Jupiter's second biggest moon. It has a surface made entirely of water ice, complete with rifts, cracks, and volcanoes that spout slush instead of lava. The tidal forces of Jupiter bend and buckle the interior of the moon, and that keeps it warm enough for liquid water to form under the ice crust. Europa's hidden ocean could be 100 km (60 miles) deep and contain three times as much water as Earth's ocean basins.

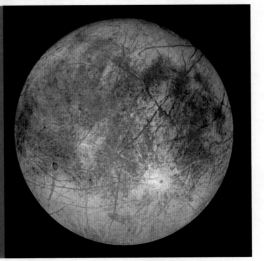

99 Ocean Cleanup

IN 1988, NOAA FIRST RECORDED WHAT BECAME KNOWN AS THE GREAT PACIFIC GARBAGE PATCH. It appeared that even the wide open ocean had become littered with plastic garbage. Thirty years later, a system to clean it up was put to work.

Developing methods of cleaning out plastic and other garbage from the ocean is one way to tackle the problem. Another is to use less plastic and ensure that it is disposed of correctly.

The Great Pacific Garbage Patch is formed by waste that has washed into the Pacific over the decades and become trapped in the North Pacific gyre. This is a circulation of currents, where ocean water slowly turns in a loop. All oceans have them, but the one in the north Pacific is particularly garbage-filled because of irresponsible disposal of plastics (mostly from Asia). The trash lies halfway between Hawaii and California, although it does not really resemble a raft of plastic spreading in all directions, as one might expect. It cannot be detected from the sky or satellite because the pieces of plastic are so small and widely spaced. Nevertheless, researchers say it covers 1.6 million square kilometers (620,000 square miles) and at its center holds 100 kilograms of waste per square kilometer. That translates as 80,000 metric tons of plastic in 1.8 trillion pieces. Beyond this garbage patch, fragments of plastic are being found everywhere from deep ocean trenches to Arctic ice.

In 2018, Ocean Cleanup, a non-profit organization, launched a prototype for sweeping up the Pacific garbage using a floating boom. It collected 2 tons of plastic in two months of real-world trials, which also showed that the system needed improvements. There are plans to deploy 60 more 2-km (1.25 mile) cleaning systems in the Pacific.

100 Planetary Science

TODAY, EARTH SCIENTISTS ARE IMPORTANT MEMBERS OF ANY SPACE SCIENCE TEAM. Their skills are used to design spacecraft that can do for other planets what earth sciences have done for our own—figured it out.

In 1960, Eugene Shoemaker showed beyond doubt that rocks in space were made of the same stuff as found on Earth (see page 99). However, the burgeoning field of space science needed no extra encouragement to go take a closer look at our neighboring moons and planets. The first interplanetary missions were flybys offering a close-up look for just a few minutes. They revealed surface features and helped to analyse the chemistry of the atmosphere. In 1971, planetary science took a big step with NASA's Mariner 9 mission, which went into orbit around Mars. The orbiter was able to map almost all of the red planet's surface revealing features such as Olympus Mons, a volcano more than twice as tall as Everest and so large it would cover Arizona, and Valles Marineris, a vast canyon system 7 km (4.5 miles) deep.

The next phases involved landers. Early attempts at Venus proved impractical—its dense, acidic atmosphere was too hostile to spacecraft—but successful missions have taken landers to asteroids, comets, and Titan, a moon of Saturn. However, Mars has been the chief focus of planetary science with several orbiters, landers, and rovers working there. Their mission is to search the Martian rocks and atmosphere for signs of water and signs of life. Perhaps human explorers will visit one day, and you can bet the team will include earth scientists.

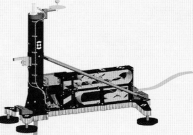

Mars InSight, which landed on Mars in 2018, has a seismometer for detecting "marsquakes," and is using a "mole" (above) to take the temperature of Martian soil.

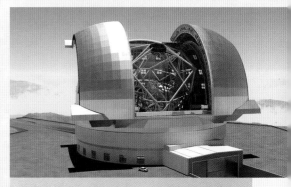

THE FUTURE

The next major mission to Mars is underway. In 2018 an orbiter called ExoMars Trace Gas Orbiter started to sniff the Martian atmosphere for methane. It is possible that this gas is produced by alien life that lives in Mars's rocks, similar to rock-eating microbes on Earth. The orbiter also tested a landing system to be used sometime in the next few years to deliver a new rover, *Rosalind Franklin* (right), to the Martian surface. Previous rovers have been equipped with tiny grinders and rock scrapers, but this rover will carry with it a 2-m (7 ft) drill for going deeper into the red planet's rocks than ever before.

SEEING EXOPLANETS

More than 99 percent of the planets we know about are not in our Solar System. We cannot see most of these "exoplanets" even with a telescope, but that is set to change with the European Extremely Large Telescope. This telescope, being built in Chile, will have a mirror 40 m (130 ft) across. Its designers say it will be able to see exoplanets clearly and even detect the chemicals in their atmospheres.

Earth Sciences: the basics

So what does all this discovery add up to? Earth sciences help us to get under the surface of our planet—and to take a tour of the atmosphere up to the edge of space. For armchair explorers, here is a roundup of the basics.

How Rocks Form

Igneous These rocks are formed when magma—a hot, liquid mixture of rock chemicals—cools down and becomes solid crystals. Magma exists deep within Earth. If it erupts onto the surface, we call it lava. The mineral composition of an igneous rock depends on the chemicals in the magma. Silicon-rich compounds are the most common. They make pale-colored rock. Darker rocks contain iron, aluminum, and other metals.

Sedimentary While igneous rocks are more common in the deep crust, about 80 percent of rocks seen on the surface are sedimentary. They are formed from clasts, or fragments of materials, such as rock grains, minerals, and chemicals that precipitate in layers. Compressed for millions of years, the clasts become glued together. Sedimentary rocks are softer than igneous ones because grains are just chemically glued together.

Metamorphic Extremes of temperature or pressure can transform the physical and chemical nature of minerals, and this transformation can change a rock into a new form: a metamorphic rock. Any rock can undergo metamorphosis: igneous, sedimentary, and even other metamorphic rocks. Usually the transformation process is so intense that it is hard to identify what the original rock was.

Making rocks A rock is a collection of other substances called minerals, and minerals are naturally occurring solid compounds. There are about 3,000 kinds of mineral, including gems such as emeralds and diamonds, plus useful chemicals like talc, asbestos, and gypsum. However, the great majority of rocks are made from just a handful of minerals, mostly composed of silicon and oxygen. While some minerals—such as the metal oxides and calcium carbonates—are formed originally at the surface of Earth, silicates are primordial substances that made up part of the young Earth. They are the major component of the magma that churns deep within Earth. The magma cools into igneous rocks. If formed at the surface, normally at the bottom of the ocean, the igneous rock will likely be a basalt, while igneous rocks that form underground are normally granite: 70 percent of continental rock is granite. These and other igneous rocks form the source materials for all the other rock types, which are created through the rock cycle, as shown below.

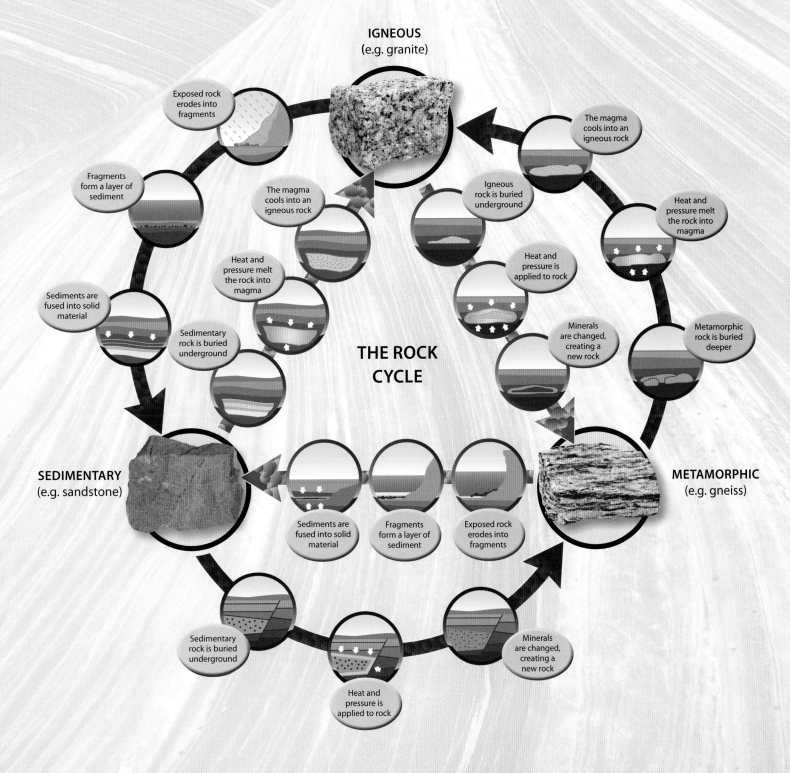

IGNEOUS (e.g. granite)

Exposed rock erodes into fragments

The magma cools into an igneous rock

Fragments form a layer of sediment

Heat and pressure melt the rock into magma

Igneous rock is buried underground

The magma cools into an igneous rock

Sediments are fused into solid material

Heat and pressure melt the rock into magma

Heat and pressure is applied to rock

Sedimentary rock is buried underground

Minerals are changed, creating a new rock

Metamorphic rock is buried deeper

THE ROCK CYCLE

SEDIMENTARY (e.g. sandstone)

Sediments are fused into solid material

Fragments form a layer of sediment

Exposed rock erodes into fragments

METAMORPHIC (e.g. gneiss)

Sedimentary rock is buried underground

Minerals are changed, creating a new rock

Heat and pressure is applied to rock

The Geological Time Scale

The great age of Earth is best expressed by the geological time scale. It divides Earth's natural history into a series of time periods, which are, from long to short: eon, era, period, epoch, and age, all of which are measured in lengths of millions of years. The divisions between them represent a global change in the fossil or rock record, and each time period allows geologists to identify rocks of the same age located around the world, and so begin to tell the history of the planet. The three columns of this time scale show only the Phranezoic eon, which covers the time since complex life appeared around 540 million years ago. Most of the rocks we see around us at the surface belong to this time. However, it contains little more than a tenth of the full 4.5 billion-year history of the world.

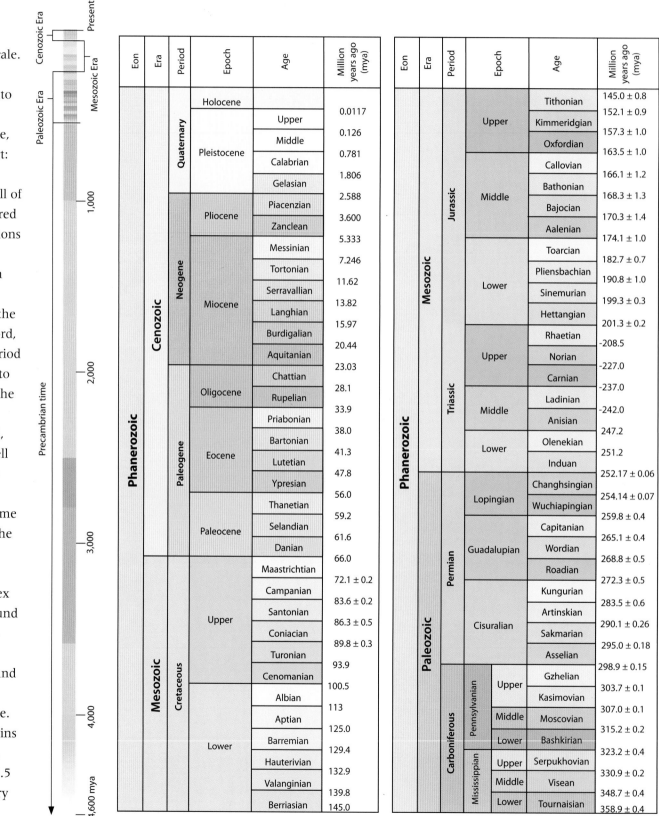

Eon	Era	Period	Epoch	Age	Million years ago (mya)
Phanerozoic	Cenozoic	Quaternary	Holocene		0.0117
			Pleistocene	Upper	0.126
				Middle	0.781
				Calabrian	1.806
				Gelasian	2.588
		Neogene	Pliocene	Piacenzian	3.600
				Zanclean	5.333
			Miocene	Messinian	7.246
				Tortonian	11.62
				Serravallian	13.82
				Langhian	15.97
				Burdigalian	20.44
				Aquitanian	23.03
		Paleogene	Oligocene	Chattian	28.1
				Rupelian	33.9
			Eocene	Priabonian	38.0
				Bartonian	41.3
				Lutetian	47.8
				Ypresian	56.0
			Paleocene	Thanetian	59.2
				Selandian	61.6
				Danian	66.0
	Mesozoic	Cretaceous	Upper	Maastrichtian	72.1 ± 0.2
				Campanian	83.6 ± 0.2
				Santonian	86.3 ± 0.5
				Coniacian	89.8 ± 0.3
				Turonian	93.9
				Cenomanian	100.5
			Lower	Albian	113
				Aptian	125.0
				Barremian	129.4
				Hauterivian	132.9
				Valanginian	139.8
				Berriasian	145.0

Eon	Era	Period	Epoch	Age	Million years ago (mya)
Phanerozoic	Mesozoic	Jurassic	Upper	Tithonian	145.0 ± 0.8
				Kimmeridgian	152.1 ± 0.9
				Oxfordian	157.3 ± 1.0
			Middle	Callovian	163.5 ± 1.0
				Bathonian	166.1 ± 1.2
				Bajocian	168.3 ± 1.3
				Aalenian	170.3 ± 1.4
			Lower	Toarcian	174.1 ± 1.0
				Pliensbachian	182.7 ± 0.7
				Sinemurian	190.8 ± 1.0
				Hettangian	199.3 ± 0.3
		Triassic	Upper	Rhaetian	201.3 ± 0.2
				Norian	-208.5
				Carnian	-227.0
			Middle	Ladinian	-237.0
				Anisian	-242.0
			Lower	Olenekian	247.2
				Induan	251.2
	Paleozoic	Permian	Lopingian	Changhsingian	252.17 ± 0.06
				Wuchiapingian	254.14 ± 0.07
			Guadalupian	Capitanian	259.8 ± 0.4
				Wordian	265.1 ± 0.5
				Roadian	268.8 ± 0.5
			Cisuralian	Kungurian	272.3 ± 0.5
				Artinskian	283.5 ± 0.6
				Sakmarian	290.1 ± 0.26
				Asselian	295.0 ± 0.18
		Carboniferous	Pennsylvanian — Upper	Gzhelian	298.9 ± 0.15
			Pennsylvanian — Upper	Kasimovian	303.7 ± 0.1
			Pennsylvanian — Middle	Moscovian	307.0 ± 0.1
			Pennsylvanian — Lower	Bashkirian	315.2 ± 0.2
			Mississippian — Upper	Serpukhovian	323.2 ± 0.4
			Mississippian — Middle	Visean	330.9 ± 0.2
			Mississippian — Lower	Tournaisian	348.7 ± 0.4
					358.9 ± 0.4

Eon	Era	Period	Epoch	Age	Million years ago (mya)
Phanerozoic	Paleozoic	Devonian	Upper	Famennian	358.9 ± 0.4
				Frasnian	372.2 ± 1.8
			Middle	Givetian	382.7 ± 1.6
				Eifelian	387.7 ± 0.8
			Lower	Emsian	393.3 ± 1.2
				Pragian	407.6 ± 2.6
				Lochkovian	410.8 ± 2.8
		Silurian	Pridoli		419.2 ± 3.2
			Ludlow	Ludfordian	423.0 ± 2.3
				Gorstian	425.6 ± 0.9
			Wenlock	Homerian	427.4 ± 0.5
				Sheinwoodian	430.5 ± 0.7
			Llandovery	Telychian	433.4 ± 0.8
				Aeronian	438.5 ± 1.1
				Rhuddanian	440.8 ± 1.2
		Ordovician	Upper	Hirnantian	443.4 ± 1.5
				Katian	445.2 ± 1.4
				Sandbian	453.0 ± 0.7
			Middle	Darriwilian	458.4 ± 0.9
				Dapingian	467.3 ± 1.1
			Lower	Floian	470.0 ± 1.4
				Tremadocian	477.7 ± 1.4
		Cambrian	Furongian	Stage 10	485.4 ± 1.9
				Jiangshanian	489.5
				Paibian	494.0
			Series 3	Guzhangian	497.0
				Drumian	500.5
				Stage 5	504.5
			Series 2	Stage 4	509.0
				Stage 3	514.0
			Terreneuvian	Stage 2	521.0
				Fortunian	529.0
					541.0 ± 1.0

Continental drift Rocks of the same composition and age are widely dispersed across the globe. This shows that although they formed in the same place, the rocks have since split and drifted across the planet. Geologists have mapped these distributions to build up a picture of how the continents have moved and changed shape over geological time. Below, we can see the continental drift over the last 380 million years, starting around the time that the first vertebrate tetrapods had emerged from the ocean and set out for life on land.

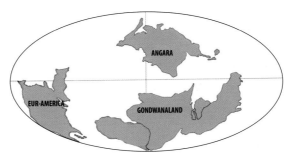

380 million years ago
The continental formations prior to this date are less well understood, but at this point in the middle of the Devonian period, Earth had three continents.

200 million years ago
By the Jurassic period, when dinosaurs and mammals were first emerging, the continents had merged, so all the land was connected in a single supercontinent called Pangaea.

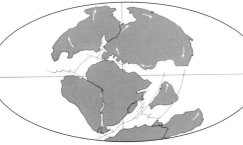

135 million years ago
During the Cretaceous period, at the height of the Age of Reptiles, today's continents were beginning to take shape and divide up.

50 million years ago
After the extinction of the dinosaurs, birds and mammals became the dominant species on Earth. North and South America were not connected at this point.

Present *Although continental drift continued, and continues now, today's geography took form around 8 million years ago, a time when our ape ancestors began to live on grasslands beyond the forest.*

Rock Identity Test

A few rocks, such as sandstone and granite, are obvious enough at first glance, but finding the identity of most rocks requires a bit more detective work. Follow this key to figure it out. You will need a magnifier, a steel nail, and a glass tile (that can be scratched).

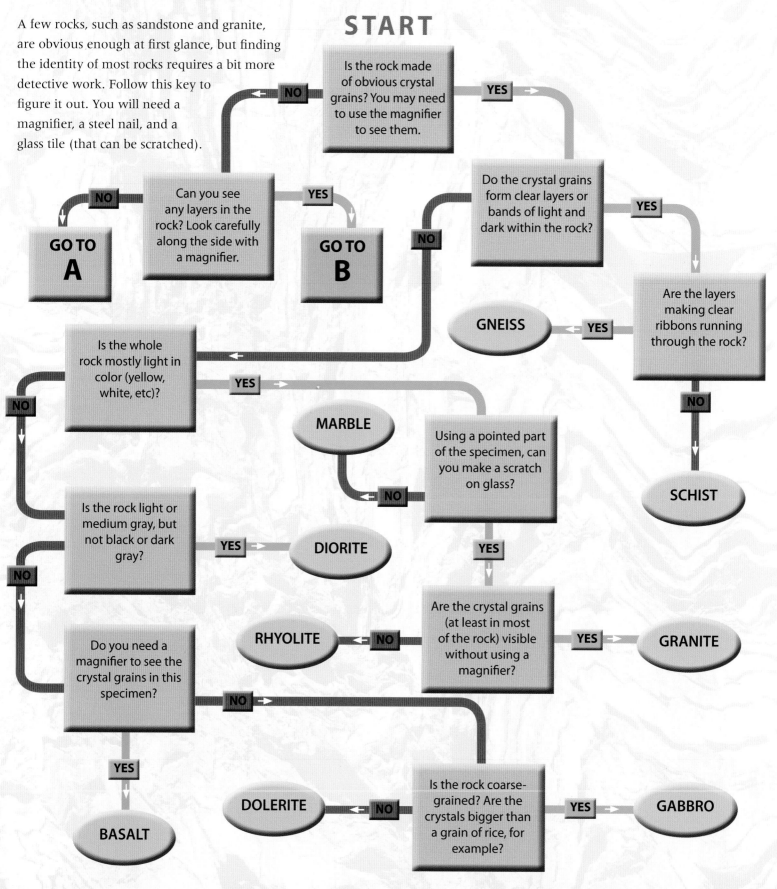

START

Is the rock made of obvious crystal grains? You may need to use the magnifier to see them.

NO → Can you see any layers in the rock? Look carefully along the side with a magnifier.

YES → Do the crystal grains form clear layers or bands of light and dark within the rock?

NO → GO TO **A**

YES → GO TO **B**

YES → Are the layers making clear ribbons running through the rock?

NO (from crystal grains layers question)

Is the whole rock mostly light in color (yellow, white, etc)?

GNEISS ← **YES** (from ribbons question)

YES → MARBLE

NO → Using a pointed part of the specimen, can you make a scratch on glass?

NO → SCHIST (from ribbons question)

NO → Is the rock light or medium gray, but not black or dark gray?

YES → DIORITE

NO → MARBLE (from scratch on glass question)

YES (scratch on glass) →

NO → Do you need a magnifier to see the crystal grains in this specimen?

RHYOLITE ← **NO** ← Are the crystal grains (at least in most of the rock) visible without using a magnifier?

YES → GRANITE

YES → BASALT

NO → DOLERITE ← **NO** ← Is the rock coarse-grained? Are the crystals bigger than a grain of rice, for example?

YES → GABBRO

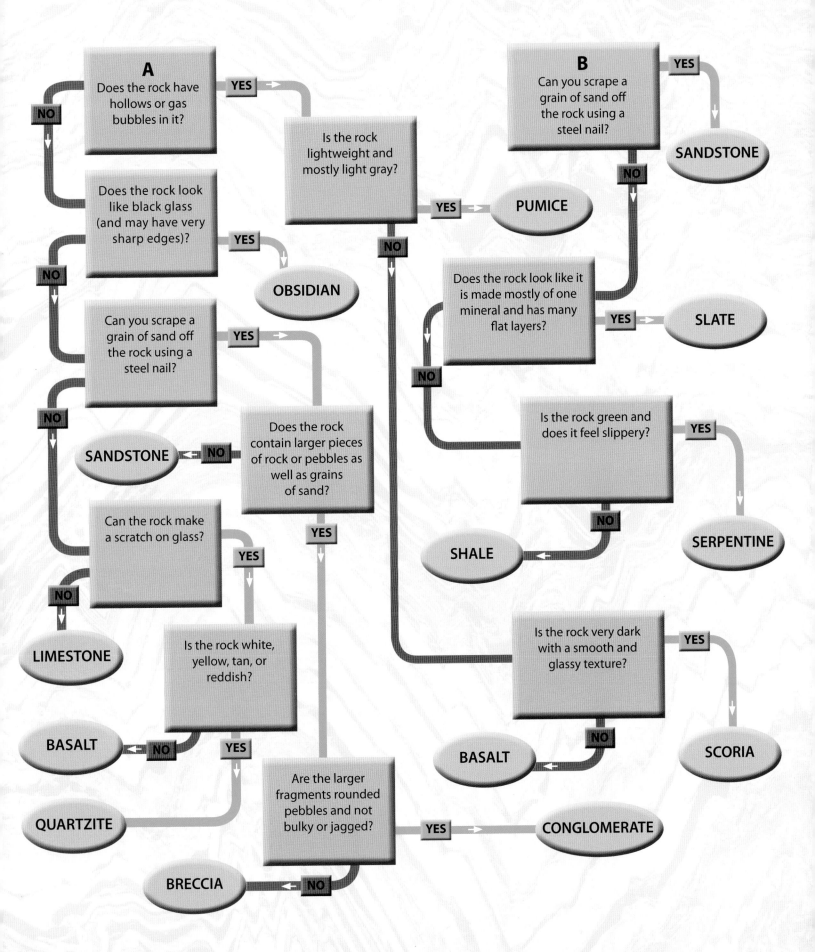

The Weather

When compared to the atmospheres around other planets, Earth's atmosphere represents two extremes. It is the most stable, with temperature always within a band ranging not much more than 100°C (212°F) from the hottest to the coldest, and the great majority of places on the surface being much closer in temperature. In addition, Earth's atmosphere is also—as far as we can tell—the most changeable. While the winds and storms on other planets might be far more severe and vast in scale, they are long-lasting and interspersed with periods of calm. Not so on Earth, where the atmosphere is in constant flux, with a great variety of conditions found from place to place. We call this ever-changing state "the weather," and knowledge of it has many practical uses in agriculture, shipping, air travel, and everyday life in general.

Cloud cover From the earliest days, people have sought to predict weather changes, and clouds were an obvious signal. Specific cloud formations are associated with the arrival of certain weather systems. The most reliable sign is that if gray clouds fill the whole sky, it is likely to rain soon! As this facetious remark illustrates, reading clouds is only reliable when the weather has more or less arrived, and any predictive power is thus diminished. Instead of decoding the clouds, meteorologists have developed technologies—observation networks, radar systems, and then weather satellites—to find out where the clouds are now, and where they are going. This information, along with other data about air temperatures and pressures, is then used to develop the forecast for where the clouds, and the weather they bring, will go next.

Cloud formations are invariably beautiful natural phenomena. They are well worth a look, despite not always being a reliable source for weather forecasting.

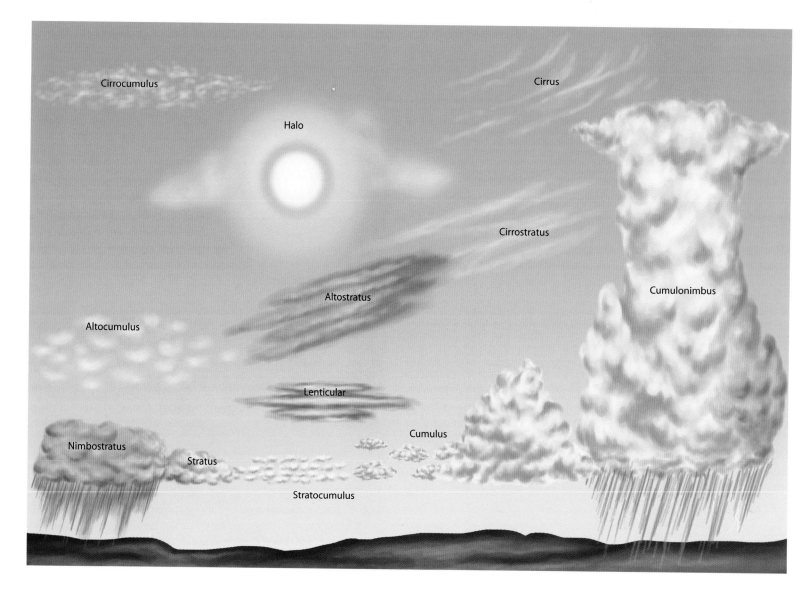

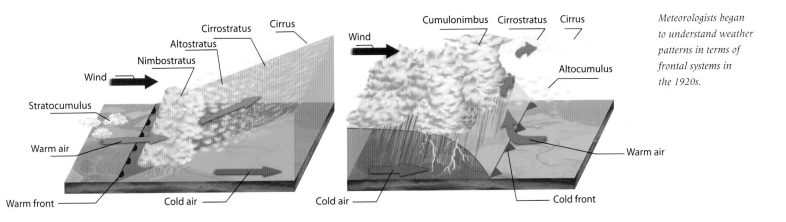

Meteorologists began to understand weather patterns in terms of frontal systems in the 1920s.

Weather fronts Weather changes are associated with the passing of a weather front, which is the leading edge of a mass of air. A warm front sees a mass of warmer air rising above a mass of cold air, pushing it away. The warm front is preceded by increasing cloud cover, possibly fog, and then a short shower from low-lying cloud. Calm and sunny weather follows behind the warm front. A cold front forces its way under the resident air mass. Behind the front, tall rain clouds loom up and create heavy and persistent rain, perhaps with thunder and lightning. If the updraft from the rising air is enough, the rain will be pushed higher and freeze into hailstones. If rain droplets fall through cold air, they will form into snowflakes.

The water cycle is driven by the heat of the Sun, which makes water evaporate into the atmosphere. Most of this evaporation occurs over the ocean, but any dissolved salts in the water are left behind as the vapor enters the air. Therefore rain is a constant and essential supply of freshwater.

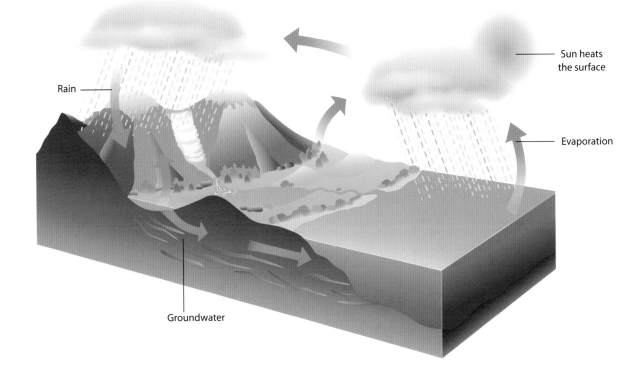

The water cycle Earth is a water planet, and the conversion of water into ice and into vapor and back again is a ubiquitous process that is important for our understanding of earth sciences. As well as filling the ocean, about one percent of the atmosphere is water vapor—although that can vary considerably—and, increasingly, geologists suspect that there is a vast reservoir of water in Earth's deep crust and mantle. The fluidity and chemistry of magma depends on its water content, and, in turn, that affects the rocks it will form. On the surface, flowing water, glaciers, and ice sheets are working to grind away at solid rock, which is a crucial phase of the rock cycle. And of course, our weather systems are driven, at least in part, by the constant cycling of water from the oceans and land into the atmosphere, then into cloud formations, and back to the surface as rain.

Climate Zones

It is possible to organize Earth's landmasses into large-scale regions that share a similar climate, thus including locations that have the same average rainfall and similar seasonal shifts in temperatures, for example. Once that is done, it becomes clear that regions in far-flung areas of the globe share the same broad climatic features. The obvious example is a desert, which is any region that receives less than 25 cm (10 inches) of rainfall in a year. The climate in turn creates a common set of habitats (and survival challenges) for wildlife to exploit. So, roughly speaking, a plant that can survive in an Australian desert has the means to do so in a desert elsewhere. Other climate regions are more or less synonymous with the natural wildlife communities that they support (as the diagram shows), and so are known by names such as grassland or forest. Fossil evidence of these kinds of habitats, along with the physical and chemical consequences of water (or the lack thereof), can show us which climate zone a rock formed in the past.

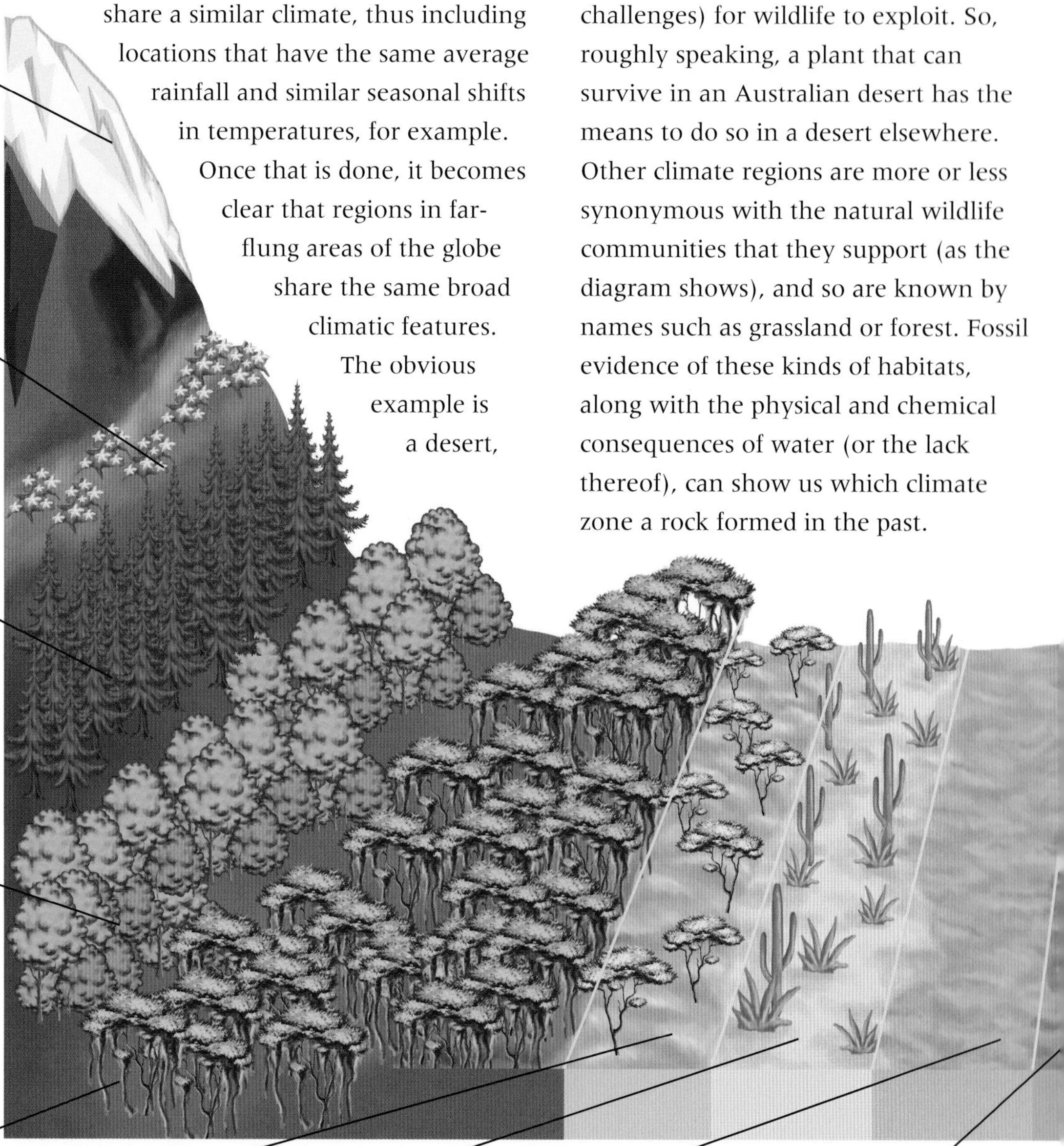

Snow line The extreme cold and high winds at the very top of the mountain give it a polar-type habitat, with snow and ice covering the ground all year around.

Tree line The upper slopes of a mountain are too cold and windy for trees to grow, and a tundra-like alpine meadow grows during the summer.

Alpine forest The air becomes thinner with altitude and so it is less able to hold heat. High habitats share a climate similar to northern forests, and so conifers are common mountain trees.

Montane forest The foothills of a mountain have shallower soils and water flows away faster than in lowland areas. As a result, forests that grow in these areas tend to have small trees.

Tropical rainforest The most fertile of all the world's habitats, these jungles grow in equatorial regions where there is high rainfall—perhaps 40 times as much as a desert—and plenty of sunshine all year around.

Tropical grassland Receiving enough rainfall, generally in a wet season, to prevent it being a desert, this habitat has tall grasses and stands of small trees. It is often better known as savannah.

Desert Since deserts receive just 25 cm (10 inches) of rain every year, desert wildlife must find and retain water to survive. While we usually think of deserts being very hot places, they also form in locations that are frequently very cold.

Semi-desert This arid habitat receives double the annual rainfall of a desert (50 cm; 20 inches) and that makes it a half-way house between tropical grassland and desert.

Shrubland Also described as heath or chaparral, this habitat has small woody plants mixed in with herbs and grasses. This kind of vegetation grows in dry habitats that are frequently disturbed by fires.

Biomes Climate zones are closely associated with the concept of bioregions or biomes. The map on the right divides the world into ten biomes, each with a distinctive set of habitats. The largest is the ocean biome, which is characterized by water, but the other nine are defined by their climates. Climate can be impacted by a local effect, such as land far from the sea being more arid than coastal areas, and high altitude regions being colder than those nearer sea level. However, a more universal factor is proximity to the Equator, where it is warmer than near to the poles.

Temperate forest
Boreal forest
Grasslands
Shrubland
Tropical rainforest

Desert
Mountain
Tundra
Ocean
Polar

Polar The polar regions are covered in ice because the temperature rarely rises above freezing. With all liquid water frozen, the polar biomes are the driest places on the planet. Along with the low temperature, this means they are also the emptiest biomes of all.

Tundra This biome surrounds the polar regions, and is largely confined to the Northern Hemisphere. Cold winter temperatures ensure that the ground is frozen permanently, so no trees can put down roots. As a result, only small, fast-growing plants, like grass and sedge, survive here by making use of the short summer to grow and produce the seeds for the following year.

Temperate grassland Forests require large amounts of water, so mild regions that receive lower annual rainfall support treeless grasslands, also called prairie, steppe, and pampas.

Temperate forest This habitat is found in regions with high rainfall, distinct seasonal changes, but a longer growing season in spring and summer. Trees drop leaves in the fall to reduce damage from winter frosts.

Mixed forest As the average temperature rises, the summer growing season becomes long enough for deciduous trees to grow among the conifers. Mixed forests also grow in temperate zones with low rainfall.

Boreal forest Also known as taiga, these forests grow where summers are too short for trees to regrow their leaves. Therefore evergreen conifers dominate, which have small, waxy needles that can withstand the freezing winter.

THE EARTH SCIENCES HAVE CHIPPED AWAY AT THE MYSTERIES OF OUR PLANET, AND REVEALED A GREAT DEAL ABOUT HOW THE WORLD WORKS. However, there are still many questions about Earth, the air, and the oceans that need answers. Let's ask a few of them.

Have humans changed Earth's geology?

Rocks are being formed on Earth's surface today from sediments in the same way as they have always been. That is the first rule of geology, right? But something has changed. The fragments of material that are feeding into the rock cycle are no longer simply rock-forming minerals recycled from other rocks or natural processes. Instead, they have materials made by humans mixed into them, things like microscopic fragments of plastic, refined oils, and radioactive metals made inside nuclear reactors—or in bombs. In a million years' time, this stuff will form part of solid rocks of completely new types that will never have been seen before.

These "unnatural" rocks (are they really unnatural?) pose no particular danger to the future of the planet. After all, the planet will persist largely unaffected by human activities. And a few thousand years' worth of unusual rock strata in there will not do much among the unimaginable spans of geological time.

Forest clearances will change the sediments that make Earth's future rocks.

A sandstone made from this beach would also contain the remains of plastics.

However, should geologists be taking more notice of them? When geologists see a global change in the geological time scale they use it as the boundary of a new epoch—or even a new period. The question is, have we humans transformed the chemistry of the atmosphere and the oceans, and altered the diversity of life on Earth so much that we have created an epochal change? The current epoch is called the Holocene, which started 12,000 or so years ago at the end of the last ice age. All of recorded human history has occurred in this latest geological epoch. There is now a school of thought that says we have entered a new epoch, and there is already a name for it: Anthropocene. That name means something like "the age of humans."

The geological jury is still out about whether to redraw the geological time scale and include the Anthropocene. The logic behind it is strong— human activity has altered Earth enough to leave a mark in its future geology. However, does geology need to take account of it right now? If it does, it would surely be mostly a signal to the world of the impact of humankind on the planet, and not a useful tool for geology itself.

The decision has been deferred by the international committees responsible for this kind of thing (the International Commission on Stratigraphy and the International Union of Geological Sciences). One sticking point is when should the Anthropocene begin? The advent of earthenware? That already predates the Holocene, so try again. The 1800s when coal mines and metal refineries began to leave their mark on sediments? While this activity has a huge impact on local soils, it is not widespread enough to constitute a global change. The favorite option for the start of the Anthropocene is July 16, 1945. This was the day of the Trinity Test, in New Mexico. This bomb test was the first nuclear explosion in history, and it left a radioactive signature in sediments across the entire globe. Nuclear weapons changed everything.

Above: Since World War II, sediments have contained tiny traces of artificial radioactive chemicals not present before.

Below: Eventually, refined steels will all rust back into natural oxide minerals.

Can the earth sciences help us control the climate?

Carbon dioxide and other greenhouse gases that are added to the atmosphere reduce the amount of heat Earth radiates out into space. This extra heat energy builds up in the atmosphere and in the oceans. What next? It is likely that the warmer conditions will drive more extreme weather, making an average storm more violent and making droughts last longer. In addition sea level will rise; partly because the ocean water will expand very slightly as it gets warmer, and that will accumulate into an overall increase in the volume of the oceans. More significantly, sea level could rise because extra water is added to the ocean as the freshwater ice caps in the Arctic, such as Greenland, melt. (By way of illustration, if all the ice covering Antarctica were to melt, the seas would rise by 60 m [200 ft], although no one suggests this will happen anytime soon.)

Would it be possible to engineer a better climate? Probably the first step is to reduce carbon emissions by using energy that does not come from burning fossil fuels. Another way might be to reduce the sunlight hitting Earth. Vast mirrors could unfold in space to reflect light away. Similarly aircraft could pump fine powders into the sky to block out light. Another possibility is suck out the unwanted carbon dioxide from the air. The gas could be extracted using chemicals, pumped underground or converted into less harmful (even useful) materials. A final suggestion is to use the ocean's "carbon pump," which is the process by which life converts carbon dioxide dissolved in the water into solid body parts, such as shells. Adding iron-rich fertilizer to the oceans would boost oceanic algae. Shellfish eat algae, so, in turn, their population would grow in number, each with a thick, carbon-rich shell, which would eventually sink to the seabed. In this way the amount of carbon dioxide in the air and water gradually goes down. Whichever path it takes, climate engineering would be the largest project in human history.

Could we engineer a way to reverse the reduction in polar ice coverage?

Every volcanic eruption and earthquake unbalances Earth a little.

Why does the Earth wobble?

Earth's axis sweeps out a circle in space every 26,000 years. That means the North Pole has not always pointed at the same patch of sky. This phenomenon, known as precession, has been understood since the days of ancient Greece. It is caused by the way the gravity of the Sun and the Moon pull on one side of the Earth slightly more than the other. When you add in the gravitational effects of Mars, Venus, and everything else in the air, the wobble becomes a complex wiggle, called nutation, that our planet makes through space.

However, there is another source of wobble called polar motion. Part of this was discovered by the American Seth Chandler in 1891, and is called the Chandler Wobble in his honor. There are similar forces that change the location of Earth's axis, so the point at the surface around which Earth is rotating varies a little every day. The North and South Poles are on the move, coiling around the officially designated points of 90° North and South and shifting about 20 meters (65 feet) every 18 months or so. This makes a small, but significant, change in precise measurements of latitude which has to be taken into account for things like GPS navigation.

The International Latitude Observatory began monitoring Earth's wobbles in 1899 to account for these shifts. (The project finally concluded in 1982, when satellite observation took over.) However, the causes for polar motion are quite hard to pin down. Some are thought to be due to the shift of huge glaciers, most notably Greenland's ice sheet, which move the planet's center of gravity. Other wobbles are likely caused by Earth changing shape as magma inside moves around. Over a time scale of years and decades, Earth's sphere is bulging, cracking, and rippling like a vast, quivering dewdrop.

Who killed the megamammals?

After the demise of the dinosaurs 66 million years ago, Earth's habitats became a level playing field, and a range of creatures competed to become the next big thing. To begin with, it looked like the snakes, lizards, and birds might win, but about 30 million years later, mammals were well and truly top dog, and top cat, and top beast in general. The Age of Mammals saw giant sloths in South America, huge wombats in Australia, and hairy rhinos and mammoths across Eurasia. However, 100,000 years ago, the average size of mammals suddenly began to reduce, first in Africa, then elsewhere. Today the average size of a mammal is half what it was back then. Around the same time, humans, including our relatives like the Neanderthals, were spreading around the world. Did we destroy all the big land mammals? Did we spread a disease that killed them all, or hunt them to extinction? Other possible factors were climate changes, which saw the planet enter an ice age around this time. Experts propose that the problems caused by humans piled up on the climate changes, making it harder for the biggest beasts to survive. Just goes to show, humans have always been making a mark on the planet.

Things were different in the past. Just ask this saber-toothed tiger and short-faced bear.

IMPONDERABLES

Is the Earth actually flat?

A survey of Americans in 2018 showed that two percent were sure that instead of a sphere, planet Earth was really a disc. The planet is not spinning, they say, and the Sun and Moon move in a circle above the disc to create daytime and nighttime. The edge of the disc is a wall of ice that keeps all the ocean water in. There is so much evidence against this idea, most of it known for centuries, that it is hard to decide where to begin in debunking it. Perhaps the simplest argument is that light travels in straight lines, and so if Earth was flat you would be able to see light coming from every point on Earth. That's right, but the mountains block our view, is the flat-earth response. In which case, wherever you are on Earth, you must be able to see mountains in the distance—but that is not always true. However, some people are drawn to the idea of a flat Earth. This is not due to a lack of intelligence (although a lack of education in earth sciences is a factor). More likely, flat-Earthers are attracted to the idea that they belong to a special group who, against the odds, are holding out against a mighty force that seeks to tell them what to think and do. Parts of that idea may or may not be true, but the earth sciences, all sciences, are a tool for finding truth, not a mechanism for deception.

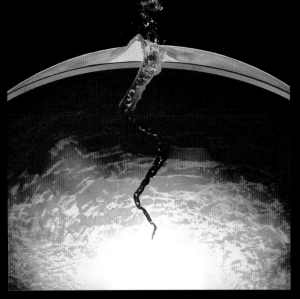

Should earth science crack open Earth to look deep inside?

Can we ever go to the center of the Earth?

Several nations have active plans to send humans back to the Moon and then on to Mars, which is a 55-million-km (34-million mile) journey, give or take. Earth scientists are not impressed. Space is decidedly empty compared to Earth. If as much attention—and money—was devoted to going down instead of up, where would we get to? As Project MoHole and others showed, traveling into Earth is just as difficult as flying to the planets—perhaps even harder, certainly for human explorers. However, Professor David Stevenson, who works at the California Institute of Technology, came up with a way of getting a remotely operated probe into Earth's core—at a cost less than the Apollo Program (although perhaps a little riskier!). His plan is this: make a crack in Earth's crust—a nuclear bomb should do it—and pour in 10 million tonnes of molten iron (which is about a week's global production). The hot metal will make the colder crust around it crack, allowing the iron to gush deeper and deeper into Earth. Stevenson calculates that there will be enough iron to slice through the mantle and reach the core. All that is needed is for a probe that can withstand the heat of molten iron (and the deep Earth). Instead of radio, the probe could tap out the data it collects on the way down (it will take about a week) as seismic waves that are transmitted through Earth's own rocks.

Are there planets like Earth out in space?

An exoplanet is a planet that exists in another solar system, orbiting a star other than our sun. The first exoplanets were discovered in the 1990s, and after the great success of NASA's Kepler space observatory mission, astronomers have now identified thousands more. In fact, it is estimated that most stars have at least one planet, and so there are more exoplanets than stars in our galaxy. (Opinions differ, but there are many billions of stars in the Milky Way.) About half of one percent of the exoplanets discovered to date appear to share Earth-like features: they are rocky and dense, and orbit in a region of their solar systems where water exists as a liquid—instead of as vapor or ice, which are much more likely states elsewhere in the Universe. Even that small percentage adds up to a minimum of 500 million Earth-like planets in our galaxy. With liquid water and the right atmospheric chemistry, these planets may very well harbor alien life forms. However, it is thought that aliens will mostly be very simple organisms, akin to our bacteria. To develop into complex life requires another set of Earth-like features, and for that life to become a space-going civilization like ours depends on a wide range of interlocking factors. For example, our sun is a quiet star that does not eject bursts of energy which would disrupt life, and our moon is enormous and is probably in orbit thanks to a very unlikely kind of collision between two planets early in Earth's history. The gravity from this large

It is estimated that there are many millions of watery and rocky planets like Earth.

moon pushes and pulls on Earth's interior, heating up the insides. That heat boosts the magnetic field created by the iron core. Our strong magnetic field keeps out nasty cosmic rays that would otherwise pose a problem for life on the surface. In addition, Jupiter, our big neighbor out toward deep space, sweeps up many of the wayward comets that might otherwise smash into Earth with an alarming regularity and cause extinctions—and prevent the long and slow evolution of civilization (that we have had). This is the conclusion of the Rare Earth Hypothesis, which suggests that while life might be common enough, civilization is very unlikely indeed, and perhaps we humans really are the cleverest things out there.

Stars are not all like our sun. Most are small and cooler, while others are too bright and prone to outbursts.

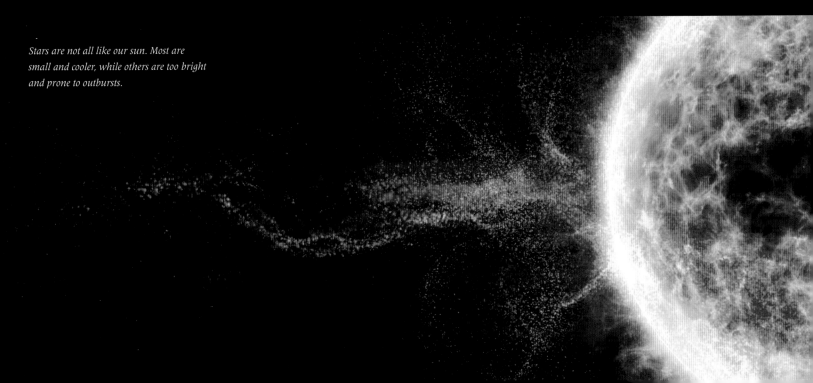

The Great Earth Scientists

THE CONTRIBUTIONS MADE BY THESE SCIENTISTS THROUGHOUT HISTORY reflect the enormous range of fields that make up earth sciences. Some have braved extremes of climate, made intrepid journeys to remote parts of Earth, or puzzled over great reams of data to find out how our planet works. Earth scientists come from all corners of science, such as astronomy, biology, and physics. Those disciplines have been put to work to reveal secrets about the deepest parts of the earth and the highest reaches of the atmosphere.

Strabo

Born	c.64 BCE
Place of birth	Amasya, Turkey
Died	c.24 CE
Importance	Author of *Geographica*

Strabo was born into a wealthy and influential family. They allied with Rome when the Persians took over his homeland in Asia Minor (what is now Turkey). As one might expect from a founding figure of geography, Strabo was widely traveled. He visited Egypt, sailing up the Nile, and went further south to the African kingdoms of Kush and Ethiopia. His westernmost trip was to Etruria (today known as Tuscany) and he spent many years in Rome itself. The date of *Geographica* is unclear, but it is thought likely to have been first written in 7 BCE. Strabo may have kept it updated right up to his death.

Theophrastus

Born	c.372 BCE
Place of birth	Lesbos, Greece
Died	c.287 BCE
Importance	Founding figure of mineralogy

As well as documenting minerals, Theophrastus had wide-ranging interests. He is best remembered for his work on plant biology, and he is often credited as being the founding figure of botany. In his two surviving botanical works, *Enquiry into Plants* and *On the Causes of Plants*, Theophrastus did for plants what Aristotle had done for animals, describing and investigating them. His scheme for classifying different plant types divided them into trees, shrubs, "undershrubs," and plants—and he also considered the medicinal properties of plants and their other uses.

Ptolemy

Born	c.100
Place of birth	?Egypt
Died	c.170
Importance	Publisher of early world map

Claudius Ptolemy was a Roman citizen who wrote in Greek, the language of the intellectual in the Roman era—ironic since Latin was the language of choice for later scholars. As well as his work on maps, Ptolemy is known for the *Almagest* star catalog. He is often styled Ptolemy the Wise to avoid confusion with the Alexandrian pharaohs that had the same name. Although he spent years in Alexandria, some authorities refer to him as an Upper Egyptian, which means he hailed from the south of the country— the Egyptian "upper' and "lower' are reversed from those expected on a map.

Al-Biruni

Born	973
Place of birth	Khwarezm, Uzbekistan
Died	c.1050
Importance	Measured the size of Earth

Many Islamic scholars built on the works of Classical Greece. Al-Biruni, who spoke seven languages and hailed from the eastern end of the Islamic world—he spent many years in what is now Afghanistan—did the same, but also found inspiration in the science of India. His main contributions were in mechanics and hydrodynamics, the motion of fluids. However, he is also remembered for calculating the radius (and therefore circumference) of Earth. To do this he used a mountain peak in what is now Pakistan to form a huge right-angled triangle with the horizon and the center of Earth.

George Hadley

Born	February 12, 1685
Place of birth	London, England
Died	June 28, 1768
Importance	Proposed mechanism of global wind system

During his lifetime, George Hadley's family was most celebrated for the work of his older brother, John, who invented the octant, a device for measuring latitude. After college in Oxford, George became a London lawyer, a career arranged by his father, and Hadley was often distracted by scientific studies. He became the chief analyst of the meteorological data accrued by the Royal Society of London. In 1735, he was elected a fellow of the society and published his trade wind theory the same year. Although his theory at first languished in obscurity, by the end of the 19th century the mechanism was known as "Hadley's principle."

Nicolaus Steno

Born	January 1, 1638
Place of birth	Copenhagen, Denmark
Died	November 25, 1686
Importance	Founder of stratigraphy

Suffering from a serious but unexplained disease as a child, Steno grew up in isolation. At 19, he went to medical school, and, once graduated, took a tour of Europe, learning from the eminent scientists at every port of call. He was particularly interested in anatomy, investigating the lymphatic system and how muscles worked. He became a leading member of the scientific society Accademia del Cimento in Italy, which is where he proposed his ideas about stratigraphy and paleontology. Around the same time, Steno converted to Catholicism, and his interest in science began to wane. He took holy orders in 1675.

John Michell

Born	December 25, 1724
Place of birth	Nottinghamshire, England
Died	April 21, 1793
Importance	Proposed causes of earthquakes

Historians of science like to think of John Michell as the most overlooked of all scientists. His contributions to optics, astronomy, and physical sciences, along with his work on seismology and earthquakes, has largely gone unheralded. Michell was the first to suggest something along the lines of a black hole, which he called a "dark star." He was also consulted by others who went on to become great scientists, such as Benjamin Franklin, Joseph Priestley, and Henry Cavendish, who is most famous for using a device designed by Michell to measure the mass of Earth.

James Hutton

Born	June 3, 1726
Place of birth	Edinburgh, Scotland
Died	March 26, 1797
Importance	Developed theory of uniformitarianism

After leaving school Hutton was initially apprenticed as a lawyer, but soon switched to being a physician's assistant, which allowed him to dabble in chemical experiments. After studying anatomy in Europe for several years, he set up a chemical business back in Edinburgh in the 1750s. At this time Hutton was also running family farms in the lowlands and highlands of Scotland. He recorded his work on the farms in an unpublished book, *Elements of Agriculture*. This farm work helped him indulge his latest passions, geology and meteorology, which occupied him for the rest of his life.

Alexander von Humboldt

Born	September 14, 1769
Place of birth	Berlin, Germany
Died	May 6, 1859
Importance	Pioneer of climatology

The son of an army officer, Humboldt and his brother were raised by their mother after their father's death in 1779. After a disinterested stab at engineering, Humboldt discovered a passion for plants and geology. In 1796 he began to travel extensively, including making an epic trip to North and South America during which he explored the Orinoco River and set a world mountain climbing record on an ascent of Mount Chimborazo in the Andes. Humboldt won great fame, and rivers, mountains, and towns all over the world were named in his honor.

Georges Cuvier

Born	August 23, 1769
Place of birth	Montbéliard (then Germany, now France)
Died	May 13, 1832
Importance	Discoverer of extinction

Georges Cuvier studied comparative anatomy in Stuttgart and worked as a tutor after graduating. He joined the new National Museum of Natural History in Paris in 1795, and soon won recognition as a leading expert on the anatomy of animals. He was reputed to be able to reconstruct the complete anatomy of a previously unknown fossil species from just a few fragments of bone. Cuvier was appointed to government positions by Napoleon Bonaparte, and continued as a state councilor under three successive kings after Napoleon's fall.

Mary Anning

Born	May 21, 1799
Place of birth	Lyme Regis, England
Died	March 9, 1847
Importance	Fossil hunter

Mary Anning, described as "the greatest fossilist the world ever knew," was lucky to have been born on Britain's fossil-rich Jurassic Coast—parts of Dorset and Devon. According

to family tradition, Anning, aged one, survived a lightning strike that killed three others. When her father died in 1810, she sold fossils to make ends meet. She struggled to get recognition for her finds, including the first plesiosaur, and, as a woman, could not join the Geological Society of London. Its members did raise money for her when she became ill, but she died of breast cancer in 1847.

Matthew Fontaine Maury

Born	January 14, 1806
Place of birth	Spotsylvania county, Virginia, USA
Died	February 1, 1873
Importance	Founding figure of oceanography

Maury was nicknamed "Pathfinder of the Seas" for his work on mapping the world's ocean currents. Starting out as a midshipman, his naval career was ended by a stagecoach accident. This began his career in oceanography with his appointment as Superintendent of the United States Naval Observatory and head of the Depot of Charts and Instruments. Following his impact on world meteorology and navigation, he was involved in setting up the U.S. Naval Academy at Annapolis. During the American Civil War, Maury resigned his commission as a U.S. Navy commander and joined the Confederacy.

Andrija Mohorovicic

Born	January 23, 1857
Place of birth	Opatija, Croatia
Died	December 18, 1936
Importance	Discovered lower boundary of crust

Mohorovicic was the son of a blacksmith. He studied mathematics and physics at the University of Prague in 1875, under Ernst Mach, who was an expert in wave behaviors (the Mach numbers for speeds of sound are named for him). Mohorovicic returned to Croatia to work as a teacher, and became interested in meteorology, marking the start of an academic career. In 1892 he became head of the Zagreb meteorological observatory, building it into one of Europe's most advanced. That year he observed a tornado pick up and throw a railway carriage with 50 people. He was an early supporter of earthquake-resistant building design.

Charles Doolittle Walcott

Born	March 31, 1850
Place of birth	New York Mills, New York, USA
Died	February 9, 1927
Importance	Discoverer of Burgess Shale fossil bed

Fascinated with wildlife and nature from an early age, Walcott did not complete high school. He became a professional fossil collector, and after meeting Louis Agassiz (a leading proponent of ice age theory) at Harvard, he decided to take up paleontology. He took a job as an assistant to the New York state paleontologist, but lost it soon after. However, his next appointment was as a geological assistant at the newly formed U.S. Geological Survey; fifteen years later he became the director. In 1907 he was made secretary of the Smithsonian Institution.

Alfred Wegener

Born	November 1, 1880
Place of birth	Berlin, Germany
Died	November, 1930
Importance	Developed theory of continental drift

After high school, Wegener studied physics, meteorology, and astronomy at various colleges. His first job was as an assistant at Urania Observatory, and he received his doctorate in astronomy in 1905. Wegener maintained an interest in the weather and climate, with a particular fascination for the polar region. In 1906 he made the first of four expeditions to Greenland. He published his theory of continental drift in 1912, although it was not widely accepted for decades. Wegener collapsed and died on a trek in central Greenland. His body was buried in the snow, and is now preserved 100 meters (330 ft) beneath the ice.

Inge Lehmann

Born	May 13, 1888
Place of birth	Copenhagen, Denmark
Died	February 21, 1993
Importance	Discovered Earth's inner core

After receiving an extraordinary childhood education from her father, an experimental psychologist, and Hanna Adler, the aunt of quantum physicist Niels Bohr, Lehmann went on to study mathematics at Copenhagen and then Cambridge. Her academic career was interrupted by poor health, and she went to work for an actuary, where she gained mathematical skills. In 1918 she started again at Copenhagen University. In 1925 she became an assistant to Niels Erik Nørlund, a geodesist (a scientist who measures Earth and its properties). He asked her to set up seismological observatories in Denmark and Greenland, introducing her to her life's work.

Charles Richter

Born	April 26, 1900
Place of birth	Hamilton, Ohio, USA
Died	September 30, 1985
Importance	Developed earthquake magnitude scale

After high school, Richter went to Stanford and started a PhD in theoretical physics from the California Institute of Technology, but before completing his studies he moved to the Carnegie Institution of Washington, D.C. It was here that he became interested in seismology, which took him to a new seismological laboratory run by Caltech in Pasadena.

In 1932, Richter collaborated with Beno Gutenberg to develop a scale to measure the relative sizes of earthquakes, which took Richter's name. Richter became a full professor in 1952. Later on in his career Richter became involved in designing earthquake-proof buildings.

Arthur Holmes

Born	January 14, 1890
Place of birth	County Durham, England
Died	September 20, 1965
Importance	Developed radiometric dating of rocks

Holmes won a place to study physics at the Royal College of Science (now Imperial College London) and switched to geology for his second year (against the advice of his tutors). He took a job as a mining prospector  in Mozambique, but found nothing and was nearly killed by malaria. In 1920 he worked for an oil company in Myanmar. Again the venture failed, and his son died from dysentery. He returned to his home county to head up the geology department at Durham University, where he began his work on radiometric dating and physical geology. He later moved to Edinburgh, and retired in 1956.

Harry Hammond Hess

Born	May 24, 1906
Place of birth	New York City, USA
Died	August 25, 1969
Importance	Leading figure in theory of plate tectonics

Harry Hess's career in academia resulted in a close association with the U.S. Navy. He made voyages on military submarines to measure the way the force of gravity changes around island chains in the ocean. He joined the navy during World War II and was made captain of the USS *Cape Johnson*, which deployed new sonar technology. Hess used this to survey the seafloor while on operations in the Northern Pacific, which formed the basis of his work on seafloor spreading  and plate tectonics. He remained in the naval reserves after returning to Princeton after the war, rising to the rank of rear admiral.

Luis Alvarez

Born	June 13, 1911
Place of birth	San Francisco, California, USA
Died	September 1, 1988
Importance	Proposed meteorite made dinosaurs extinct

Along with his son, Walter, Luis Alvarez was the driving force behind the 1980 theory that the dinosaurs were wiped out by a meteorite strike. However, this was just the final chapter of an incredible career. In the 1930s he began working as a particle physicist and discovered a radioactive form of hydrogen called tritium. That saw him becoming part of the Manhattan Project during World War II, where he developed the detonators for nuclear weapons. After the war, Alvarez developed bubble chambers that could track subatomic particles which were crucial for the discovery of many new particles. He won the Nobel Prize for that work in 1968.

Ted Fujita

Born	October 23, 1920
Place of birth	Kitakyushu City, Japan
Died	November 19, 1998
Importance	Developed tornado strength scale

Beginning his career at the Kyushu Institute of Technology, Fujita was living in Kitakyushu in 1945. This city was meant to be the next target to be hit with a nuclear weapon after Hiroshima, but due to cloud cover, the second bomb was dropped on Nagasaki, instead. In 1953 Fujita was invited to continue his work at the University of Chicago, where he extended his theories about violent rainstorms called downbursts and microbursts and also developed the Fujita scale of tornado intensity. "Mr. Tornado," as he became known, also helped to develop ways of observing tornadoes and surveying techniques to assess damage.

Marie Tharp

Born	July 30, 1920
Place of birth	Ypsilanti, Michigan, USA
Died	August 23, 2006
Importance	Discovered Mid-Atlantic Ridge

Marie Tharp took music and English at college with a view to being a school teacher. However, World War II opened up opportunities in male-dominated professions, and she joined the petroleum geology program at the University of Michigan in Ann Arbor. After a brief stint in the oil industry, she became an assistant at Columbia University's geology lab. There she worked with Bruce Heezen to create seafloor maps. Tharp pieced together several pieces of data to discover the oceanic rift zone, a theory that was at first not widely accepted.

Mario Molina

Born	March 19, 1943
Place of birth	Mexico City, Mexico
Died	–
Importance	Discovered the ozone hole

As a child, Molina created a laboratory in a bathroom at his home, fitted out with toy microscopes and chemistry sets. His aunt Esther, a chemist, helped him with his experiments. He studied chemical engineering at the National Autonomous

University of Mexico, and went to Germany to earn a postgraduate degree in polymerization kinetics. From there he went to Berkeley, and published his work on CFC gases with Sherwood Rowland in 1974. Following the success in 1987 of the Montreal Protocol to protect the ozone layer, he won the Nobel Prize in 1995 and dozens of further awards.

BIBLIOGRAPHY AND OTHER RESOURCES

Books

Allaby, Michael. A Dictionary of Geology and Earth Sciences. 2013.

Alley, Richard. The Two-Mile Time Machine. 2000.

Alvarez, Walter. T. Rex and the Crater of Doom. 1997.

Anderson, Robert S. and Suzanne P. Anderson. Geomorphology: The Mechanics and Chemistry of Landscapes. 2010.

Bell, Jim. The Earth Book. 2019.

Benton, Michael and David A. T. Harper. Basic Paleontology: Introduction to Paleobiology and the Fossil Record. 2009.

Broecker, Wally and Charles H. Langmuir. How to Build a Habitable Planet. 2012.

Burbank, Douglas W. and Robert S. Anderson. Tectonic Geomorphology. 2011.

Cherrix, Amy. Eye of the Storm: NASA, Drones, and the Race to Crack the Hurricane Code. 2017.

Christiansen, Eric H. and W. Kenneth Hamblin. Dynamic Earth: An Introduction to Physical Geology. 2014.

Gohau, Gabriel. A History of Geology. 1990.

Gould, Stephen Jay. Wonderful Life: The Burgess Shale and the Nature of History. 1989.

Grotzinger, John P. and Thomas H. Jordan. Understanding Earth. 2010.

Hawking, Lucy and Stephen Hawking. George & the Blue Moon. 2016.

Hazen, Robert M. The Story of Earth. 2012.

Knoll, Andrew H. Life on a Young Planet: The First Three Billion Years of Evolution on Earth. 2003.

Lamb, Simon and David Sington. Earth Story. 1998.

Littell, Mcdougal. Earth Science. 2005.

Lockwood, John P. and Richard W. Hazlett. Volcanoes: Global Perspectives. 2010.

Longstaff, Alan. Astrobiology: An Introduction. 2014.

Lutgens, Frederick K. and Edward J. Tarbuck, Dennis G. Tasa. Foundations of Earth Science. 2016.

MacKenzie, W. S. and A. E. Adams, K. H. Brodie Rocks and Minerals in Thin Section: A Colour Atlas. 1994.

Mathez, Edmond and James Webster. The Earth Machine: The Science of a Dynamic Planet. 2004.

McPhee, John. Annals of the Former World. 1998.

Nield, Ted. Supercontinent. 2007.

O'Hara, Kieran D. A Brief History of Geology. 2018

Redfern, Martin. The Earth: A Very Short Introduction. 2003.

Reynolds, Stephen and Julia Johnson. Exploring Earth Science. 2015.

Searle, Mike. Colliding Continents. 2013.

Spooner, Alecia M. Geology For Dummies. 2011.

Time-Life Books. Planet Earth. 1997.

Walker, Sally M. Fossils. 2008.

Waltham, David. Lucky Planet: Why Earth is Exceptional – and What that Means for Life in the Universe. 2014.

Zalasiewicz, Jan and Mark Williams. The Goldilocks Planet: The 4 Billion Year Story of Earth's Climate. 2012

Museums

Academy of Natural Sciences, Philadelphia, PA, USA

American Museum of Natural History, New York City, USA

Australian Museum, Sydney, Australia

Beijing Museum of Natural History, Beijing, China

California Academy of Science, San Francisco, USA

Canada Science and Technology Museum, Ottowa, Canada

Carnegie Museum of Natural History, Pittsburgh, PA, USA

China Science and Technology Museum, Beijing, China

City of Science and Industry, Paris, France

Deutsches Museum, Munich, Germany

Field Museum of Natural History, Chicago, IL, USA

Geological Museum of China, Beijing, China

Hungarian Natural History Museum, Budapest, Hungary

Indian Museum, Kolkata, India

Jurassic Coast Museums, Dorset, UK

La Plata Museum, La Plata, Argentina

La Specola, Museum of Zoology and Natural History, Florence, Italy

Lee Kong Chian Natural History Museum, Singapore

MUSE, Science Museum, Trento, Italy

Museum of Natural History, Berlin, Germany

Museum of Natural Sciences, Brussels, Belgium

Nairobi National Museum, Nairobi, Kenya

National Coal Mining Museum, West Yorkshire, UK

National Museum, Rio de Janeiro, Brazil

National Museum of Natural History, Madrid, Spain

National Museum of Natural History, New Delhi, India

National Museum of Natural History, Paris, France

National Museum of Nature and Science, Tokyo, Japan

National Science Museum, Pathum Thani, Thailand

Natural History Museum, London, UK

Natural History Museum, Vienna, Austria

Natural History Museum of Denmark, Copenhagen, Denmark

Olduvai Gorge Museum, Ngorongoro Conservation Area, Tanzania

Ontario Science Centre, Toronto, Canada

Origins Centre, Johannesburg, South Africa

PaleoWorld Research Foundation, Jordan, MT, USA

Proyecto Dino, Lake Barreales Paleontological Center, Neuquén, Argentina

Royal Tyrrell Museum of Palaeontology, Drumheller, Alberta, Canada

Science Center NEMO, Amsterdam, Netherlands

Science Museum, London, UK

Science Museum, Tokyo, Japan

Shanghai Natural History Museum, Shanghai, China

Smithsonian Institution, Washington, D.C., USA

State Darwin Museum, Moscow, Russia

Te Papa Museum, Wellington, New Zealand

Universeum, Gothenburg, Sweden

Wyoming Dinosaur Center, Thermopolis, WY, USA

Yuri Orlov Palaeontological Museum, Moscow, Russia

Zigong Dinosaur Museum, Sichuan, China

Archives and Preserved Equipment

Bathyscaphe Trieste, U.S. Navy Museum, Washington D.C., USA

Darwin Papers, University of Cambridge, UK

Down House, Charles Darwin's home, Downe, Kent, UK

T. Theodore "Ted" Fujita Collection, Southwest Collection/ Special Collections Library, Texas Tech University, USA

Arthur Holmes Papers, Durham University Archives, UK

Alexander von Humboldt papers, Berlin State Library, Germany

Gideon Mantell papers, National Library of New Zealand, Wellington, New Zealand

Matthew Fontaine Maury Papers, Virginia Military Institute Archives, USA

NASA's Intrepid Sea-Air-Space Museum/Space Shuttle Enterprise, New York, USA

Charles Richter papers, California Institute of Technology, USA

Charles Doolittle Walcott Collection, Smithsonian Institution Archives, USA

Alfred Wegener Archive, Bremerhaven, Germany

Other Places to Visit

Baradla-Domica Cave, Hungary-Slovakia

Carlsbad Caverns, New Mexico, USA

Cave of the Crystals, Chihuahua, Mexico

Chicxulub Crater, Chicxulub, Mexico

Eisriesenwelt (World of the Ice Giants), Hochkogel Mountain, Austria

Dinosaur National Monument, Colorado, USA

Grand Canyon National Park, Arizona, USA

Institute of Oceanography, Nha Trang City, Vietnam

Jeita Grotto, Jeita, Lebanon

Jeju Island Lava Tubes, South Korea

Jenolan Caves, Blue Mountains, Australia

Mammoth–Flint Ridge Cave System, Kentucky, USA

Meteor Crater, Arizona, USA

Mulu Caves, Gunung Mulu National Park, Borneo

Perito Moreno Glacier, Patagonia, Argentina

Petrified Forest, Lesbos, Greece

Reed Flute Cave, Guilin, China

San Andreas Fault, Carrizo Plain, California, USA

Scripps Institution of Oceanography, California, USA

Skaftafell National Park, Iceland

Škocjan Caves, Divača, Slovenia

Stromboli Volcano, Stromboli, Italy

Uluru, Northern Territory, Australia

Waitomo Caves, Waitomo, New Zealand

Wieliczka Salt Mine, Wieliczka, Poland

Woods Hole Oceanographic Institution, Falmouth, Massachusetts, USA

Yellowstone National Park, Wyoming/Idaho/Montana, USA

Websites

British Geological Survey, www.bgs.ac.uk

European-Mediterranean Seismological Center, www.emsc-csem.org

Incorporated Research Institutions for Seismology, www.iris.edu

International Union of Geological Sciences, www.iugs.org

The James Hutton Institute, www.hutton.ac.uk

Khan Academy, www.khanacademy.org

NASA Earth Science, https://science.nasa.gov/earth-science

National Oceanography Centre, UK, www.noc.ac.uk

The Nobel Prize, www.nobelprize.org/educational

UNESCO's International Geoscience Program, www.unesco.org/new/en/natural-sciences/environment/ earth-sciences/international-geoscience-programme

U.S. Geological Survey, www.usgs.gov

World Meteorological Organization, https://.public.wmo.int/en

Apps

Cloud Labs, pbs.org

Earth Now, NASA

Earthviewer, hhmi.org

Glossary of Geology, American Geosciences Institute

iGeology, British Geological Survey

iQuake Lite, Orion Microsystems

Mineral Database, Mindat.org

World Atlas, National Geographic

INDEX

Cataloging-in-Publication Data has been applied for and may be obtained from the Library of Congress.

ISBN: 978-1-62795-141-8

Series Concept and Direction: Jeanette Limondjian
Design: Bradbury and Williams
Editor: Meredith MacArdle
Proofreader: Julia Adams
Picture Research: Clare Newman
Consultant: Dana Caccamise
Cover Design: Igor Satanovsky

Publishers' Note: While every effort has been made to ensure that the information herein is complete and accurate, the publishers and author make no representations or warranties either expressed or implied of any kind with respect to this book to the reader. Neither the author nor the publishers shall be liable or responsible for any damage, loss, or expense of any kind arising out of information contained in this book. The thoughts or opinions expressed in this book represent the personal views of the author and not necessarily those of the publishers. Further, the publishers take no responsibility for third party websites or their content.

SHELTER HARBOR PRESS
603 West 115th Street Suite 163
New York, New York 10025

For sales in the USA and Canada, please contact
info@shelterharborpress.com

For sales in Europe, please contact
info@worthpress.co.uk

For sales in the UK, please contact
sales@manningpartnership.co.uk

Tom Jackson is a science writer based in the United Kingdom. Tom specializes in recasting science and technology into lively historical narratives. After almost 20 years of writing, Tom has uncovered a wealth of stories that help create new ways to enjoy learning about science. He studied at the University of Bristol, UK, and still lives in that city with his wife and three children.

Printed and bound in China by Imago.

10 9 8 7 6 5 4 3 2 1